MY *Mother* ONCE TOLD *Me...*

Carol A. Schauer

WITH HELP, AS ALWAYS, FROM
MOM, BARBARA J. ASHWORTH

My Mother Once Told Me...
Published by Fannie Press
Denver, CO

ISBN: 978-0-578-75687-5
Personal Memoir
Cover and Interior design by Victoria Wolf, Wolf Design and Marketing

Without question, without pause, without taking a breath,
I dedicate this book to mothers and daughters.

I dedicate a large portion of this book
to my mother's writing.

In letters, in stories, in keepsakes, she gifted
me in writing them down.

INTRODUCTION

I'VE RECORDED AND WATCHED *Dr. Phil* every day. I've watched his show and, prior to that, his appearances on *Oprah*, for over two decades. He has said, "The greatest role model in a child's life is the same-sex parent." I can't count the number of times he's stated those words. So many! In most instances, his guest is a parent who is falling short in parenting their son or daughter. Clearly his intent is to remind his guest of their biologically determined, requisite role in their child's life. Surely he's offering encouragement and motivation to improve the behavior they are modeling. Be it good or bad, or accepted or rejected, that modeling influence has already been planted. For example, Dr. Phil has spoken of his father's drinking and conversely of his own abstinence from alcohol. We can connect those dots.

I get it. Even though I didn't recognize this power in my life until well into adulthood, my mother's influence, once cemented, once cured, often in the blink of an eye, cannot be taken back.

When I think of my thought processes, my value judgments, my perspectives in general, and even my speaking cadence, it is clear they are patterned after my mother. It is almost unnerving. I think it would be *definitively* unnerving if I didn't like my mom—but I do. Even when my perspective or actions are in contrast to hers, the learned behavior of obstinacy can rear its ugly head.

Neither my mom nor I had awareness of this influence in the first twenty-plus years of her mothering. We just went about the tasks, triumphs, and tears of life, her being a mom and me being a kid, oblivious to the subliminal lessons being taught and learned. Somewhere between thirty and forty years old, I began to allow thoughts of when my mom wouldn't be around. Allowing those thoughts awakened me to the multitude of times in any given day when her influence surfaced.

The thoughts crept into the most mundane of activities. It was when I did the things my mom did. When I'd sew or clean house or when I'd make a pie crust from scratch. If I heard a church choir or watched a movie musical, I would instinctively sense her opinions entering my mind. During the years I was pondering these esoterically mystical thoughts, my mother began to speak more often about her own mother. I was beginning to see the lineage. These mother-daughter influences go on and on, generation after generation. This experience is universal, whether actions, words, or experiences present the information consciously or unconsciously.

What about fathers? What about sons? And what about people who lost their mothers too early or never knew their mothers to begin with? Well, I can't speak to that. I can't speak to how that void is filled or how another unconditionally loving being can compensate. I know it happens, but I simply can't speak to it. In fact, I can't speak to anything other than my mother's mother, my mother, and myself, and the first is primarily through the telling from my mom. It's a direct line: Fannie, Barbara, and me. This, I can speak to.

I

I'd Like You to Meet ...

THREE WOMEN:

a mother, a daughter, and the daughter's daughter. I am the latter. I am nothing if not my mother's daughter, as her influence is the single greatest driving force in my thoughts. Who are we, if not our thoughts? Regardless of our actions or our outward presentations, we are first our thoughts.

Abraham Lincoln is quoted as saying: "All that I am, or ever hope to be, I owe to my angel mother." I can honestly say no consistent human presence or even inconsistent subtle influence explains who I am, *other* than my mother. Of course, that is not all good. Perhaps I should have had some valuable paternal or extended family influence. I didn't. And most certainly, all that glitters isn't gold, as my mother wasn't without her flaws, some of which I consciously or unconsciously mirror.

For the record, I had both a biological father and a stepfather. I lived in a family structure with my stepfather from age two to twenty-two. Those two opportunities for a nurturing paternal influence were pretty much black holes. My stepfather was in the US Navy; therefore, we moved every two years on average. The chance of long-term influential relationships with extended family or mentors was simply nonexistent.

I'm not saying I always think or act like my mom; I don't. And I am not without highly dramatic diversion from her behavioral tendencies. I have thirty years of escaping lasting consequences by the skin of my teeth, from some reckless decisions and actions, most of which were contrary to her tendencies. I *am* saying my gumption, my independence, my strength of will, my "can do" spirit, my work ethic, my tolerances, and probably my intolerances, can all be linked to her past and her past's past.

An intangible, imperceptible process exists within my mind that reaches back before my life and gathers the experience of both my mother and grandmother. Perhaps it's from storytelling, or those defining, split-second moments of maternal guidance, but there's something more Ouija board happening, something more biological or cosmic or Divine. The span of time is a mere three generations, technically calculated at sixty years. More accurately, more than one hundred years have passed since time encased my grandmother's birth, my mother's birth, my birth, and today.

The lives of my grandmother Fannie and my mother, Barbara, are remarkable, absolutely remarkable, and certainly only recognized as such in retrospect. I have both benefitted from and abided their influences. If I'm strong (all who know me would say yes), if I'm independent (that's rhetorical), if I'm stubborn (whoops, my slip may be showing), all is attributable to who came before me. Whatever is good in me, I credit my mom, and whatever is good in her, we credit her mom.

FANNIE PHOEBE

(Waterbury, Ashworth) Schmidt, my maternal grandmother.

Fannie Waterbury was born on August 20, 1888, in Baca County, Colorado. The town listed on her birth certificate was "rural" and the place listed was "at home." She was the fifth of eleven children born to Victor Newton Waterbury and Rosella (Rosa) J. Smith Waterbury. All children were born one-right-after-the-other from July 1881 through July 1899. Nine of the Waterbury children lived lengthy lives. The sixth born, a son, was killed in WWI at age twenty-three, and the seventh, another son, lived only fourteen months.

To align the times with some historical context, Robert LeRoy Parker, later known as Butch Cassidy, was born a mere eight years before Fannie. By 1896, he and his gang of outlaws were wreaking havoc throughout Utah, one state to the west of Colorado. If I hazard a guess, surely less notorious but no less dangerous outlaws traversed the eastern plains of Colorado. Get the picture? It's almost incomprehensible to connect those old cowboy times and my grandma.

The six Waterbury girls, if I believe the folklore, were coveted brides. They came from "healthy stock." They were hard-working and knew how to work a farm, a home, and bear children. All the girls were of average height, maybe five foot, four inches, all had average physiques, and all were strong and fit.

One can trace the Waterbury line back to Stamford, Connecticut, in 1649, and further back to John Waterberye, circa 1560, in Sudbury, England. Ancestor Count Warmund von Wasserburg can be traced to Bavaria, 1010 AD. Another piece of folklore includes the Waterbury clan coming to America on the Mayflower—"right along with all the other crooks and convicts," as my mom would say.

Fannie's "at home" birth took place in a covered wagon on the open prairie, as her family with four children under age seven was en route to stake a land claim in eastern Colorado. Three years later, having failed in the venture, with now six children under the age of ten, the family journeyed back east to Belle Plaine, Kansas. By the time Fannie was five, the family took part in the "Pioneers of the Cherokee Strip" land rush in Oklahoma. Just as you'd see in an old Western movie, the family and their possessions, consisting of two wagons loaded with household goods, a tent, a chicken coop, and a pig in a box, with six children ages twelve to three walking beside the wagons herding the cows, traveled westward to make a new home.

How Fannie met and married Charles Ashworth was unknown to my mother, and she never thought to ask—until too late. Fannie's youngest sister, Lyda, wrote an account of the family, including events before she was born. Within the pages of her writing, Fannie is barely mentioned. Probably a proverbial forgotten middle child, as she and another sister drop off the story entirely. It's possible both took off with traveling salesmen who came through Oklahoma looking for wives. It's also possible they took off on their own, seeking better lives for themselves. Regardless, given the hard-life, rural circumstances and the fact that Fannie was nearing twenty-six years old, perhaps the term "slim pickins'" applied to her choice of husband. Fannie married in 1914 and bore two sons shortly thereafter. They lived as farm hands, and Fannie cooked for the entire crew. However, sometime in the early or mid-1920s, they moved to California to seek a better fortune.

Fortune was not to be had, as Charles was a drunkard. Their daughter, Barbara June, was born in 1927. Fannie did all she could do to be the breadwinner for the family since Charles seldom held a job for any length of time. She worked in a sewing factory, but the whirring of the machines made her so nervous, she was allowed to be a presser. Of course, this meant she was on her feet all day long. Additionally, she cleaned offices at night, took in laundry and ironing for others, and worked as a mother's helper, helping more fortunate women care for their children. She just worked, all the time.

As a mother, she did her best to provide for her children and protect them from the traumas and damages suffered while living with an alcoholic father. Her efforts were undoubtedly limited by her lack of education, the Great Depression, and societal norms of being a housewife and mother. Jobs were scarce and compensation was scant.

She supported her children emotionally, believing in them, which built their confidence. Her sons left the family by the time they were in their early and middle teen years. They'd had their fill of living in poverty and suffering abuses from their alcoholic father and thought they could do better on their own. The oldest joined the military as soon as he turned seventeen. The younger did the same once he was old enough. Their decision pained Fannie, as she'd done her best to provide and protect them, yet it wasn't enough. She chose to always support her children's decisions. If she herself had a choice to leave with her toddler daughter, she didn't know it. She stayed—working and protecting her last child.

Charles died of alcoholism in 1940. While the exact cause of death is unknown to me, alcohol consumption surely hastened his demise. Fannie's sons were long gone. Now it was only her and Barbara June. Both worked at any job they could get to support their lives. At fourteen, Barbara June was sent to clean for others or earn loose change as a mother's helper. In a letter to me, much later in her life, my mother, Barbara June, wrote about this experience.

I remember when I was fourteen or fifteen and worked as a moth-er's helper one summer and had to live at their house. She had four kids; three years old, eighteen months, and two-month-old twins. I would lie in bed at night and yearn to go home. I thought the time would never pass when I could quit. It wasn't a fun job.

Astonishingly, Barbara June's best friend in junior high school, Idean, came to live with them for two years. Fannie was a widow, with no means and a young teenage daughter to support, yet she took in another child so the girl would not have to live in a group home. Idean is now grown, and a great-grandmother herself, and speaks of Fannie's kindness with heartfelt tenderness. It's possible Idean's father offered some form of minimal support, but given that he also suffered from the consequences of "the drink," I can't be certain of such details.

Fannie and Barbara June attended church regularly. Faith was a constant. Idean recalls a lady from the church providing them various forms of assistance: clothing, food, or payment for simple chores, but these occurrences were rare, as the women were embarrassed and reluctant to accept charity.

At age fifty-three, Fannie met and married a widower, Henry Schmidt. While not wealthy by any stretch, Henry provided Fannie and Barbara June with the very first house they could call their own. The structure was a shack, easily a building at risk of being condemned or uninhabitable, but it became a home far and away better than any place they'd ever lived. They moved it to a vacant lot, added a front porch, and made some improvements.

I remember that house. Part of my memory is from the story my mom would tell of my grandmother making pancakes. My mom told me that when I was about three years old, I ran past the stove, counting the pancakes, "Two, four, *sickit*-eight, ten!" I don't remember the counting, but I do recall running out the back screen door as I passed the stove and hearing the door slam behind me and my mother and grandmother laughing as I went outside to play. I also recall another visit, perhaps a year later, when I saw a little figurine of Three Monkeys. I asked my mom what it was, and she explained, "Hear no evil, see no evil, speak no evil." I loved those monkeys and the message. I keep a similar small figurine beside a photo of my mother and grandmother.

Fannie was seventy years old by the time I was three. Henry had passed on and she was an old woman. Seventy is not that old by today's standards, but her life was relentlessly burdened with hard physical work and hardships of survival. She looked old.

I have heard from my mother of Fannie's boisterous, energetic, laughing, engaging personality. But I never observed it. Mom spoke of how Fannie's outspoken behavior embarrassed her. Regrettably, she handled her embarrassment as most teenagers would: she was nasty and dismissive of Fannie and Henry. I'd have loved to have seen that extrovert side of Fannie; I only remember her being quiet.

In 1966, Fannie had changed her life again. With no assistance, no family counsel, no help at all, she disposed of her home and meager possessions and moved herself into a nursing home. Her oldest son had died in 1962, and her younger son had abandoned her, for all intents and purposes. He was married and had two children and lived in the same area of Southern California as his mother. But he made little or no effort to visit her, let alone offer any assistance.

Within a year, my mother and we four kids visited her. She had a room with a twin bed and a dresser. The surroundings were sterile, with linoleum tile floors and pale, yellow walls. My grandmother was dressed in her best dress, the only dress I'd ever seen her wear, in person or in photos. Other residents were in housecoats, daily-wear robes, so I can assume she dressed up for the occasion of our visit. I recall us all walking the hall, much slower than any kid wants to walk, while she loosely held on to the hand rail. Old, frail people sat in wheelchairs, just outside the doors to the many rooms along the hallway. Mom had told us, in advance, to be quiet.

My mother asked, "Do they treat you well?"

My grandmother replied in a quiet, even tone, "Yes, yes, they do."

I'm sure we had many more conversational exchanges, but this is the only one planted in my memory. I didn't know what to make of it, at eleven years of age.

My grandmother Fannie lived her life with integrity, with honesty, with joy, with resilience, with laughter, with independence, and with pride in her children, especially her daughter. With only her wits about her and a third grade education, she survived the difficulties that came her way. Her daughter benefited from and assumed her strengths and her "can do" spirit and passed it all on to me.

BARBARA JUNE ASHWORTH,
my mother.

She was born in Santa Barbara, California, on June 5, 1927, considered a later-in-life child, as her mother was thirty-nine years old. Fannie and Charles Ashworth's two sons were already in their early and mid-teens by the time the baby girl was born. Before

Barbara June turned three, the boys had escaped the family. Barbara June was called by her middle name, June, for the first twenty-eight years (and beyond, by those who knew her then) and Barbara for the bulk of her adult life. I called her Mom.

She used to say, "I was poor-white-trash before it had a name." She said this with humor, with intent to dismiss the poverty and fragility of her childhood. She seldom wanted to talk about the chronic hardships and deprivations of her childhood. But once in a while, she'd tell some story, and the listener's response would urge her to continue. Her stories were never to garner sympathy. She spoke of the startling, often barely believable, instances and events with a matter-of-fact, no-nonsense truth-telling. Listeners were always intrigued and glued to every incredulous word. She was telling about her life, her experience. She was not telling a sad sob story.

Often, she was the "tough guy" in her own life story, sometimes the self-deprecating butt of the joke and sometimes the unsuspecting underdog. But she was never the victim. Internal fortitude was her strong suit. For decades, she focused on anticipation of and protection from any threat or full-blown evil. A threat could be as mild as her thinking someone was acting superior toward her. She called it "acting the snob." An evil was the frequent risk of bodily harm. Much later in life, when threats and evils were far in the distance, people simply recognized and criticized her strong suit as stubbornness. It was impossible for her to change the patterns that had worked efficiently for her for so long. Poor? Yes, she was. Trash? Not for a second.

June lived in Southern California until she was thirty-one years old. Early in her life, she and her parents lived in the slums of southeastern Los Angeles—long before the area was referred to as "the hood." It was the slums or skid row before it was the projects. They moved a lot, within just a few miles, even just a few blocks. They moved because they didn't pay the rent. Because evictions always followed nonpayment of rent, she attended six different schools in the first grade. She graduated from Pomona High School in 1945.

June was married twice. The first marriage was in November 1947 and lasted until the end of 1955. She synopsized the dissolution of the marriage by saying, "I just wasn't going to live like that." The second marriage was in March 1957 and lasted until 1978, unofficially. The divorce was finalized six years later. She bore four children, two from each marriage, two daughters and then a son and daughter. I am the second of the first two daughters.

June entered junior college right out of high school. In 1945, junior college was basically free, a somewhat automatic advancement after high school. During her second marriage, she continued her education with night school—college courses taught for adult continuing education. During my early elementary school years, I recall her going to school one night a week. When her second husband's naval career led us overseas, she took correspondence courses. One in particular was a famous writer's course. She wanted to be a writer.

Education pursuits continued throughout the 1970s, inclusive of earning her bachelor of arts degree in journalism with a minor in French when we lived in a small town in southwestern Minnesota. June, who by this time in her life was called Barbara, worked as a real, true journalist on the small town newspaper. She was so proud.

She had a career. She told me, "I have a college degree and a position that requires one."

She had spent the bulk of her adult life as a mom and military wife, chauffeuring us kids, cooking, cleaning, and re-establishing all of our lives every couple of years with the next military tour of duty. My mom continued her education, receiving her master's degree in journalism from North Texas University at age fifty-eight. She completed all coursework for her doctorate degree by age seventy-two, but stopped short of submitting a dissertation. At the time, she told me she didn't care about the degree; she just liked going to school, learning. She also said, "Every PhD I've ever met was a snob, and I don't want that. I don't ever want to be that way." She never was.

She held various jobs while unmarried; she was a secretary and she worked in a department store. Then, with her college degree, she worked on the local newspaper, and in her early sixties, she taught a couple of journalism courses at Texas Christian University for a semester or two. During the lengthy process of her second divorce, she found her role as a Mary Kay beauty consultant. The company professed: "God first, family second, career third." She proudly represented the product for thirty years, always seeking the burst of success that would put her in a higher income bracket. That, or winning the Publishers Clearing House Sweepstakes!

I have no singular photographic image of my mom in my head. I've seen so many photos, and I've looked at them all countless times, so give me any geographic residence or time in her life, and I can pull up an image from my memory. She was a very pretty young girl with blonde, shiny hair and small, true-blue eyes. Her mother adored her. In Fannie's eyes, everything June did was better than anyone else could do it, case closed. She was the quintessential apple of her mother's eye.

As she entered adolescence, she developed a curvy, hourglass figure; wide in the hips and solid in her thighs. She would challenge that description, saying, "That's putting it nicely. I was fat!" She was not tall; she peaked at five foot two inches. Her blonde curls had darkened to a soft, medium brown, and she always took great care with her hair. She set it in pin curls every night throughout high school. Her hair was a coveted attribute; unfortunately, it became lifelessly thin and fine by midlife. Her nose was petite, stick-straight, and perfectly centered on her face. Her chin and jaw were geometrically square. In her mid-thirties, she looked a little like the Hollywood star Debbie Reynolds from the same era.

She was athletic in her youth and continued athletic challenges throughout her life. She took up ice skating at almost forty years old. She rekindled her childhood tap dancing in her seventies, performing in a troupe of senior ladies for better than a decade. Without much stature, she struggled with her weight, compounded by giving birth four times and the onset of middle-age spread. She was usually a size twelve—sometimes she'd peak above a fourteen—and like most women with weight issues, she kept that one pair of "Laura Petrie white ankle slacks" in her dresser drawer for fifty years, reminding her to get back to a size eight.

Perhaps most unique, she had a voice. She could sing, and sing well. She sang in school, she sang in church, and my sister told me she sang hymns on a Sunday morning radio program. She even made a record once. She was assigned the lead in almost every school musical production. The only time she wasn't was when a teacher would default to a lesser talent in the spirit of fairness. She sang at every girlfriend's wedding. The song "Always" was most popular, and June sang it at Idean's wedding. She was in every choir or small-group singing opportunity that crossed her path throughout her life. In high school, her voice was a primary source of self-confidence, but not conceit or egotism. She sang because she loved to, not because others gave praise. When her mother attended a performance and would stand up clapping, point to the stage, and shout, "That's my girl!" June would cringe. Such outspoken behavior was uncommon for women at the time, but that was Fannie. Like any adolescent, June was embarrassed by her mother's bold, loud behavior. Years later, she recognized it as her mother's unbridled support for her singing ability.

Her defensive bravado was well known; she seldom let down her guard, and she was a take-charge gal. Those who knew her then and those who knew her in her eighties would resoundingly agree. She wasn't a bully, she didn't push others around, but she was clearly "no-nonsense, get the job done, do it right, and don't whine about it." Those same tactics were employed on us kids.

ME.

I was born on July 15, 1955.

I like my birthdate; I like all the fives. My mother had her twenty-eighth birthday one month earlier, and my sister had just had her third birthday. We lived in National City, California, just outside San Diego. Within the first months of my life, my parents divorced, and sometime shortly after, my mother, sister, and I moved to nearby Chula Vista, California. Four months shy of my second birthday, my mother met and married my stepfather. My brother was born ten months later, and another sister was born four and a half years after him. Who I am within my sibling structure has paramount importance in my self-perception. I'm not the oldest; I'm not the youngest; I'm not the lone boy. I fit in the family structure as a second born, middle child.

I am loud. Well, not so much *always* loud, but my voice always carries, be it loud or soft. "Talks too much to her neighbors" was frequently written on my elementary school report cards. Sometime in my twenties, I learned the word *gregarious*. Yes, I like the sound of that word. One who enjoys the company of others—I looked it up. Cows are gregarious in choosing the herd versus a solitary existence. While I wasn't particularly thrilled with the reference to cows, I understood the concept. Though my mom was quick to criticize my excessive talking and loudness, she laughed when telling the memory of me at five years old, following her into the bathroom, hauling a kiddie-chair so I could sit and continue my chatter while she bathed. She also would offer praise for my ability to join a group of people and make all feel welcome, even unconsciously seeking out the most timid so as to make them feel comfortable.

I am the tallest of the women in my family, at five foot nine inches. People would look at me and glance back and forth from my mother to me and wonder how she had me. My height began to surpass hers by the time I was in sixth grade. It's easy to like being taller now, but I didn't like *not* being the cute, petite cheerleader-type through my teen years. I was not the cheerleader-type, as I'm not particularly coordinated, and I don't have those perfect cheerleader-looking legs. I have wanted *great legs* all my life, but I don't have them. I have skinny, shapeless calves with larger ankles, thick feet, chunky knees, and average thighs and hips. Oh, and let's just put icing on the cake with the development of varicose veins by the time I was in high school! On the positive side, my legs get me where I need to go. I've never had a waist, in fact, at age eleven, my measurements were 28-28-28, a great source of humor to my curvaceous mother. All my genetic physical likenesses lean strongly to the paternal side.

Weight fluctuations have been a chronic theme. I'm usually ten to twenty pounds overweight, but on three occasions in my adult life, I've surpassed that barrier by another thirty pounds. My mom teasingly called me The Three Sizes of Eve, mocking the 1960s movie, *The Three Faces of Eve.* Let me just say, figuratively, three women are living in my house, and each has access to a bedroom closet. That skinny gal, the one who's at her desirable weight, can really spend money on clothes! The other two try to spend money, but usually end up with outerwear, shoes, or handbags—as when nothing else fits, I can always find those. And with my thick feet, if I find shoes that fit, I buy them. I buy them all—with little concern for need or personal restraint. I may need them *some*day. Living in a four-season climate, sandals and boots garner equal obsession. I'm not kidding. Imelda Marcos has nothing on me. I think it's an illness, an undefined syndrome of some kind, but new shoes can always cure the blues.

My best physical feature has always been my hair. It's uncommonly thick, a little coarse, full of body, and grows fast. It does have a forceful growth pattern, which is often annoying, but I'd still prefer my hair to most other options. My worst feature early in life was my teeth. It was evident by the time I was two years old that I needed corrective measures. I had three front teeth instead of the normal two, both in my baby teeth and permanent teeth, as well as alignment issues. Oral surgery began at age six, followed by retainers to begin the multiple processes. By age twelve, I'd endured more surgery and four years of orthodontics, including a neck brace apparatus. Top that off with more surgery to remove my five (yes, five!) wisdom teeth at age eighteen. The photos I see of my bio-father confirm my bad luck in also inheriting his teeth genetics.

Given our family's military income level, the corrections might not have been possible had my issues been less complicated. The corrections were deemed "non-cosmetic," therefore "medically necessary" and partially covered by the military health benefits. Grateful does not begin to express my appreciation. I don't care how talkative, energetic, happy, and gregarious I was; at some point, the ugliness of my teeth would have had unyielding influence over my outward projection and changed the course of my life. Every little kid is cute if only because of their individuality in behavior or appearance. I was always smiling, always enthusiastic and tenderhearted. However, when looking at my mid-childhood photos, still smiley and enthusiastic, I see the proverbial "face only a mother could love."

I am reasonably smart, reasonably bright, reasonably witty, reasonably quick, reasonably educated, and reasonably successful in my career. Reasonably successful speaks to a solid middle-class life, owning my home and owning the freedom of middle-class financial means. I do take pride in having arrived at that place all on my own. I am more independent than any woman I've ever personally known. That just happened. It was definitely in my maternal role model and possibly in my maternal genetic line, if such is passed through the gene pool. To my thinking, the actual making of a decision to be an independent, single person never happened.

In my twenties, I recall thinking, "Well, I'd like to be married by age twenty-six." That sounded like a good number—then it came and went. So I thought twenty-eight sounded good, or before I'm thirty, or thirty-five. And the next thing I knew, I was thirty-six and had never been in a post-college, adult romantic relationship (I had worked like a man possessed!). I was unhappy in my job, feeling horribly unloved and unlovable with no children to spread my joy in all things "kids," and to top it off, I was nearing one of those weight peaks. For thirty-six years, I had made choices consciously and unconsciously that brought me here to this place of not being happy with my life or myself.

My lifeline was my mom. She welcomed my visits, she loved me, and my emotional dependency on her was obtuse, out of balance, whacked. Secretly, I was burdened with thoughts of: *How could I be, if she ever wasn't around? Who would love me?* Fear of losing her became a vice around my heart, causing actual physical pain. My "reasonably quick" told my "reasonably bright" this was not "reasonably smart" thinking. I sought guidance. I needed to know how or why I chose the paths I did, so I could make changes. Friends and family were unaware of my desperation, probably because I rarely exposed anything less than happiness. However, it was real, it was painful, and I needed help to remedy it.

Choosing to put it all out on the table, I should also say I'm marginally attractive. I'm not pretty, or striking. Now in my sixties, I've become one of the invisible women of our society, but I was never one of the noticeable ones anyway. I'm not vain or absorbed in my appearance; I'll head to the grocery store in my yardwork clothes, sans makeup or futzing with my hair. However, when I put forth a little effort and choose flattering clothes, I'm okay.

Unfortunately, that good feeling of, "Hey, I'm not so bad" is destroyed once a photo is taken, and I see nothing I like in the picture. More often than not, just when I have reached a desired weight or have purchased a particularly special item of clothing, once a photo appears, my momentary positive self-image takes a hard blow. Usually, I toss that clothing item in the give-to-charity bin, or seek a new hairstyle, or start a new diet, or … eat some potato chips and dip. I learned this self-deprecation from my mother—she would agree, as she struggled also. I have a bad habit of pointing out my flaws. I'd rather openly confess them than risk anyone thinking they'd discovered them, and I was oblivious.

I try to be a good daughter, sister, aunt, boss, and friend. Of course, I'm not without my shortcomings, but my intent, my heart, is always in the right place. With full disclosure, I am not and have never been married. I used to feel defensive about being single, and my defense looked an awful lot like angry offense. I fell into thinking there had to be something wrong with me. However, regardless of how I feel now, the stigma is still out there in our culture. Being a self-supporting, "never married" woman versus being a divorcee sparks speculation and assumptions that can still hurt my feelings.

I am not a lesbian and I'm nauseated to think I may be referred to as an old maid or spinster. I believe a number of good men are out there, but not as many as there are good women. At times, my criticism toward men has been harsh, but not without reason, and I often have unreasonably, unfair expectations of men. My single status has less to do with not liking men and more to do with lacking trust in them, fearing control from them, and not being chosen by them. Multiple experiences and spoken or unspoken messages have formulated this self-analysis.

And I do not have any children—not for lack of wanting or trying.

When it comes to my work, I feel genderless most of the time. I cannot escape working with, for, or supervising men, even if I wanted to. But I don't. There are a number of men I have liked, respected, and highly valued in my work life—a huge number. The difference was that none of them assessed me, or their like of me, on account of my being female. Male work associates who brought physical feminine attributes into their evaluation of me are not in the likable group. This also includes those who were ignorantly patronizing or insinuated I didn't belong because of my gender, or the worst, assessed my skill as less because my style or method did not come from a man's perspective, regardless of achieved results.

I manage people in the hospitality industry, specifically in restaurants, for a living. The work is a "do for others" business, and I'd like to claim I am a servant leader. I entered college with intent to be an elementary school teacher. I'm gifted with an uncanny rapport with little kids; I never met a kid I didn't like. That rapport is reciprocated, as somehow kids just know they are safe with me. Working in the restaurant-bar business during college sparked the switch to hospitality management after the first year.

As my career winds down, I can recall every individual who would speak praise for a positive impact I may have had on an aspect of their life. I also know there are those who'd speak the contrary. My memory plays tricks with me, recalling my worst moments of poor judgment and my most triumphant, joyful affirmations of appreciated leadership. That ratio has swung to the left and swung to the right through the past forty-five years of my supervisory roles. In the final tally, with vigilant efforts to improve, the good side will reign heavily.

I like many aspects of my choice of career. It's highly gregarious. We welcome all people. It's not "rocket science." Performance is judged on good common sense, work ethic, energy, honesty, and an aptitude to serve others. Restaurant work is an industry that can take a minimum wage worker to median income within a four-year span of time. Bring the skills mentioned before, add a desire to learn and a reasonable level of intelligence, and I'll help you get there.

Like my grandmother Fannie, I can talk to anyone, I laugh easily, I can engage others, I am protective of children and a champion of others, I am one who "does for" versus one who is "done for." I keep my eye on the exit door; I always have a plan.

Like my mother, Barbara, I am stubborn, I have insecurities about my appearance, my armor appears thick (but the skin is paper-thin), I'm intolerant of those who do others harm, I scorn any elitist behavior, and I relish a job well done. Like both my mother and grandmother, I am infinitely resourceful and my strength comes from depending on myself.

I am who I am, in large part because of my mother and

grandmother. My choices, my fight-or-flight instincts, my harshness, my kindness, my judgments, my roller-coaster self-confidence, my independence, strengths, and weaknesses are rooted in the values and experiences observed or told by these two women. My mother's words and behaviors were rooted in her mother's values and experiences. All were planted in me. While each individual brings a composited DNA and free will, those roots are still present. The apple doesn't fall far from the tree.

II

On

Writing

LOVE, MOM

June, aka Barbara, aka Mom, wrote letters, lots of letters! Ninety percent of her letters were typed: first on a manual typewriter, then on one of those heavy-duty IBM electric typewriters, and finally on her computer. She handwrote letters only when she was sitting in a car repair shop or a hospital room or someplace away from home. From as early as I can remember, she wrote her mother every week and always enclosed a self-addressed, stamped envelope for Fannie's reply. I asked her why she did that and she told me, "Just to make it easier for her to write back."

Without much first-person knowledge of my grandmother, I found this strange. What's so hard about addressing an envelope and putting a stamp on it? Once, I recall reading a snippet of a letter from my grandmother. Her third grade education was evident in her writing. *That's* why Mom provided the envelopes. She would never voice criticism with regard to her mother's lack of education. Providing the addressed envelope, postage attached, assured the safe delivery of Fannie's letters to her.

Barbara was beginning to feel regrets for not doing more for her mother, not being there, not caring for her. Barbara's resources weren't grandiose, by any stretch. She didn't have extra money floating around to send to her mother, and her military-wife status prohibited a geographic closeness. The gesture was a simple kindness, a simple courtesy, an attempt to do for her mother. On rare, intermittent occasions, she'd enclose a five-dollar bill with the letter. Once we moved to New Zealand with my stepfather's navy assignment to Operation Deep Freeze, Antarctica, this practice became more of a necessity, as international postage was more expensive and complicated. But the pattern continued until her mother, Fannie, died while we were living in Virginia in July 1967.

My mother also wrote letters to friends and extended family. While living in New Zealand, she wrote of our excursions and unusual, out-of-the-country experiences to all friends and family members. One in particular was a couple from our prior residence in Stockton, California. They were parents of my older sister's best sixth grade friend. Most of my folks' friends were other military families. The military is a subculture, a private club, allowing people of all backgrounds, ethnicities, and religions, with one thing in common: the military. This couple was not military. They were smart, well-read, college educated, and to my mother's admiration, honorable, nice people. Ten years *after* our three-year tour of duty was completed, four cross-country moves later, and upon the occasion of Barbara earning her BA in journalism, those letters were returned from these kind friends in a manila envelope with a handwritten note of appreciation, praise, and encouragement to become a writer. Mom kept it forever. While I know my mom wrote letters because it was the only means of long-distance communication available, she also enjoyed the practice—the writing of her thoughts and descriptions of events for the joy of the reader.

She wrote individual Christmas greeting letters to well over eighty people and families. Form letters or copied letters were not her choice until many, many years later. And even then, she always added a personal note to each. Military families meet a lot of people. The number of names in the address book increases with every relocation.

On the rare occasion when my stepfather was stationed as active duty, either aboard ship or overseas away from the family, they wrote each other daily. *Every* day! Both of them numbered the envelopes, just a tiny number on the back, at the point of the glued-down flap. That way, if the letters arrived out of sequence, they could keep them in order.

And, she wrote me letters. And I wrote her letters. I learned this habit well. Today, I write my friends far more than they write me. I also enjoy the telling of a story or event and the intensity of thought it takes to relay the telling well. I also keep a large address book; I don't like to let people slip away. This is an unspoken lesson from my mom. I saw her pleasure, bordering on obsession, with her daily "check for the mail," especially at Christmastime, and it seeped into my psyche. Today, I feel the same about email, as people rarely write and mail letters, seeming to prefer the immediacy of email. My mom never felt the same about email. She'd go days, possibly a week, without checking email, but she would scold the mailman under her breath if he was thirty minutes past his expected delivery time. She would annoyingly discard the junk mail onto the kitchen counter with a flick of her wrist or light up with excitement at receiving a letter.

The first real, stamped letter I wrote her was when she left our home for a few days and traveled from coast to coast to handle the needs of her mother's passing. I was twelve years old. She kept it. I wrote consistently one college summer when I chose to work in Maryland, away from our home in Minnesota. And then, once I graduated college at twenty-one years of age and naively, fearlessly moved to Chicago to begin my career in the restaurant business, we wrote each other prolifically. She saved all those letters, and I now have them. I was often scolded for failing to date my letters.

At the time, I ignored her repetitive complaint as I didn't grasp the importance. I didn't know she was saving them. Today, I have to try to sort the letters chronologically by the postmark, if legible, or the return address, if she kept the envelope or the content.

Our letters were sometimes specific to an upcoming event or family gathering; on occasion, they were with intent to relay a sorrow or troubling circumstance or life dilemma, but the vast majority of them were simply a day-in-the-life. I wrote of my work with passion and pride, relaying challenges and triumphs, and she was keenly interested. She wrote of her friends, our family, and various tasks on her to-do list. We both wrote with loving words of appreciation for each other's presence in our lives.

She kept large, cardboard storage boxes in a closet in her house, a box with each kid's name on it, containing the cards and letters we'd sent through the years and perhaps a couple of schoolwork mementos. My box was the fullest, even though my siblings' boxes also held notes sent from their children. Mom always said I talked too much and this was proof. Regretfully, I didn't have the foresight to save her letters until 1983, a full six years after I struck out on my own. I'm certain she talked me off a few cliffs in those early adult years.

To my thinking, even if it's rationalizing, my gift of gab was not the primary reason for the quantity of letters. I had seen her and her mother write to each other weekly for many years. I was just mirroring the behavior. Besides, as I synopsized in another letter more than three decades later, she was my closest confidante for my entire life. I told her just about everything. While yes, there were communications from each of us that remained confidences with our respective best friends, through our letter writing our closeness grew. I was entering fully independent, career-focused, single adulthood, and she was unwillingly thrust toward fully independent, newly divorced, empty-nest adulthood.

When I was feeling lonely or sorry-for-myself aloneness, I would open my floral patterned storage box reserved for such keepsakes and reread her past letters. She had an unknowing habit of changing her salutation in almost every letter.

For my twenty-eighth birthday, July 1983, she ended her letter with:

You know that I hope your birthday is special to you. Outwardly you voice differing points of view about birthdays. One year you talk about how birthdays are more important than Christmas since it's a personal holiday – and then the next year you wish the day could be skipped over lightly. It is a special day—I'm not talking about the (number of) years since that's something you can't do anything about so there is no point in fretting about them – it's special to me because I remember when you were born (I'm the only one who can really remember that so that makes it special). I wish it were possible for me to recall every little detail of your life, but it's not. But I do recall that you have always been a joy to me and I love you dearly,

Have a Happy Birthday

Love, Mom

I can grab any letter, any year, and take myself down to a puddle on the floor, wallowing in her expressions of love for me in her salutations:

Take care of yourself, eat right, and get enough sleep and tell yourself each day that your mother loves you.

Take care, my love, and try not to become so frustrated in your job that you hurt yourself.

Thanks for being such a sweetie. I love you with all my heart.

I love you, dear one.

I just wanted to write you a note to tell you how much I love you and how much I appreciate everything about you.

Thanks for the boots the wallet, and the guardian angel. Now I have a constant symbol of you – my true guardian angel.

I can hear my mother's voice (from my mouth) as I say, "Now I ask you—does it get any better than that?" (Pass me a tissue.)

These loving salutations were not what I grew up hearing from her. Ours was not a hug-and-kiss family; we did not speak loving words to each other. We were taught manners: to say please and thank you, table manners, and respect to adults. But no "I love you" was being said, no hugging was going on. Many people of my generation can relate to this. Subsequently, most baby boomers swung the pendulum strongly in the opposite direction when raising their own children. Receiving these letters was an about-face paradigm shift. A decade or more later, my mother displayed much more freedom in her verbal expressions of love to us, but it began for me in writing, in the letters.

I think if asked, "Why the change?" she would say, "There was so much going on ... keeping you kids in line, trying to keep (husband) happy, I just didn't think about it, and there was never time to think about it."

Then, while I might phrase the question without attack, without any blame, she would still hear it as a criticism. The knot in her throat of hurt feelings would last only a second, though, replaced by the more familiar emotion of "mad."

"It's always my fault ... you kids always blaming me." But even this had softened by the time she was in her sixties. Now, this would be said with a little grin, a little glimpse of self-awareness.

At the time of my twenty-eighth birthday letter, she was intently focused on trying to remain positive during the damaging, embarrassing, demoralizing, and hurtful events of her second divorce. Ever resilient, always with the strength of the Rock of Gibraltar, she defaulted to her crutch and wrote of her anger toward her soon-to-be ex-husband. In a face-to-face moment with me, she once spoke of how hurt she felt to be told she was no longer wanted. Sparked by her experience, this letter also contained a simple passage of advice:

A passing thought ... in looking for a husband make sure that you find someone that strives to do something to make you happy each day – not one who strives to make himself happy each day.

My box of letters, to and from my mom, is a cherished possession. Years ago, I'd reference her letters to feel her presence, her
voice, her guidance, and her love. Now, I find comfort in simply
knowing the box is there. It's available to me whenever I want, but
I don't indulge in reading often. They are there, at my beck and call,
just as my mom was.

ONCE IT'S WRITTEN

My mother once told me, "Once it's written, it's there forever,
you can't take it back."

Throughout her adult formal education, Barbara wrote stories.
She wrote assignments encompassing whatever style or direction
was being asked by the teacher, and she chose events from her life as
the subject matter for the vast majority of her short-story writing.
With pride, she kept many of those writings. And, while she didn't
resubmit a previous work to a new instructor, she often rewrote a
prior story, seeking to improve from the feedback she'd received.
Most often, she wrote of her personal experience from a first-person
perspective, thereby documenting her life. Her stories stuck to the
facts within her memory. If she presented emotion, it was barely a
bullet point versus an expanded thoughtfulness.

But when she wrote inclusive of others, our family or friends,
she often used different names. Once I absorbed the first couple of
paragraphs, the connection between the names of the characters
and the real-life story became clear. This was her way to protect
others' privacy.

Her storylines strayed on occasion, ever so slightly here or there, toward a fictionalized version of the actual event. It's possible, with regard to some occurrences, my memory or perspective is just different than hers. We all process memory input in coordination with the maturity and experience we possess at the time. Surely, my siblings have different perspectives than mine, yet we all grew up in the same family. Their memories and stories were implanted with their own emotion, maturity, and perspective at the specific moments in time. My memories are not always the gospel; they're just mine.

The composition of my mother's stories is different than the composition of her letters, and I prefer the latter. Mom said she struggled with letting go in her story writing. Her need to protect herself and others prohibited her abandonment of inhibitions or boundaries to just let it rip from her gut. Furthermore, she was not a gossip. Privacy for herself and others was a guarded boundary. She articulated her restraint when she said, "Once it's written, it's there forever. You can't take it back." Her caution is detectable in her story writing.

She tended to present her adult self as the voice of reason and logic, and therefore she was right. She was not romanticizing her self-image; she truly believed herself to be such. Others were often wrong, lacking good judgment, or "a kook," as she would say. She did not present herself as the June Cleaver type, the high-heeled, pearl-wearing mother, but simply as the stable, logical force.

Grammar and spelling were priorities to her, in speaking, letter writing, and stories. I was a lousy speller as a kid, but not now. Oh, I *am* grateful for computer spellcheck, but my hard copy dictionary is always close at hand—the one she gave me for Christmas sometime in my twenties. *Sit* and *set* compared to *lie* and *lay*. I hear, "I'm going to sit down" versus "I'm going to set down" exactly as I hear "I'm going to lie down" versus "I'm going to lay down." Very few people hear this incorrect use of the word "lay." My friends have grown weary with my constant correction. I should just shut up about it, but I *am* my mother's daughter. Also, the past tense of "sneak" is "sneaked," not "snuck." But you'll hear public speakers, newscasters, and teachers use the word "snuck." This word is prominent for me because she had two top-of-the-list intolerances: "I can't stand a sneak—a sneak or a fibber!"

Whenever any of us erred grammatically, she corrected us. Always. Language was her passion; broadening her vocabulary, speaking, or writing well was always in pursuit. Barbara did not use foul or offensive language, ever, and chose to live her life without exposure to such language. This was a clear line of demarcation. A new acquaintance of hers, a slightly younger woman somewhere between our ages, used the word "shit" on occasion. My mom felt compassion for this newly divorced gal and invited her to Christmas dinner that year, in 1990. The woman used the word at the dinner table, and I watched as she attempted to engage me through eye contact as a co-conspirator in what was socially acceptable. I didn't bite. I knew better in my mother's home. I knew my mother didn't allow such language. Sure enough, within a few weeks, Mom told me she had to tell the friend, "I don't allow that language in my life, so if you choose to use those words, I cannot be your friend."

My mother's life-long friend, Idean, tells a similar story. In high school, Idean tended to use the word "damn." June would hit or pinch her every time she said it, effectively breaking her of the habit. June was a force to be reckoned with, as this memory is still clear and prominent to Idean, seventy-some years later.

One day in my senior year of college, I was in the car with Mom. In relaying some event, I used the term "pissed off." She scolded me, "Carol! Don't use such language!"

I replied, "Well, men do," probably thinking I could sneak in her mental back door with an argument that would appeal to her occasionally voiced position on women's equality.

However, she one-upped me in replying, "And aren't we better?"

The twelve-word exchange has stayed with me. She urged me to develop a vocabulary with alternative words to convey the most offensive of the swearing options.

Once (or fifty times, at least) while playing cards with the family, including my young nieces and nephews, I said, "Oh crap," disgruntled with the hand I was dealt. Again, I was scolded; *not* in my mother's house.

Now, I confess, I have not always followed her advice outside of her presence. I have been vile, I have been crass, and I have brazenly anted-in or led foul-mouthed conversations in my life. The restaurant/bar business can be a bit raw, not always, but certainly often. In a business world, where frequently I was the only female at the conference table, I thought displaying such brashness was my way into the culture of men. I sensed most men on edge (or maybe it was only me on edge), trying to figure out the new restrictions my being there presented. I assessed that if they thought I was an impediment to their club, they would never accept my presence.

Once I'd let a few choice phrases rip, they all seemed to calm down, laugh, and let me in. Oh, I'm sure I could have taken a higher road, but I didn't know where it was.

Today, I may have found the onramp to that road. While I do choose to seek a broader vocabulary, I also choose to curse on occasion. I differ from my mom, though, in not choosing to let the crass language of others be a point of no return with friendships. For me, that would be "gosh-darn" hypocritical. I just don't sweat it. However, I'd be lying if I didn't acknowledge my admiration for anyone who is well-spoken and presents a broad vocabulary, free of swear words.

Near the beginning of one of her many writing courses, Mom wrote of her internal quandary when writing. She didn't presume to have expertise on any topic and never wanted to sound like a know-it-all. She also knew she had unique experiences and circumstances. She knew she was smart, but wrestled with where boundaries might lie. Her self-protection patterns had been established long ago.

Is it really possible for a housewife to learn the craft of writing and turn this writing into profit? Am I presumptuous to think I could write something that might be of interest to others? These questions have plagued me for quite some time and have intensified since I began studying with the Famous Writers School. My husband is in the Navy and we've traveled

to foreign countries and lived in different sections
of the United States, including Hawaii. We've made
many friends through our travels and continue this
friendship through letters. Each move with the family
brought its own peculiar set of problems and experiences. Many times as something interesting or exciting
has happened I've tried, unsuccessfully, to inscribe
the event in words so glowing and descriptive that our
friends would be able to see and feel the experiences
through my letters.

Nevertheless, even though I felt these were badly
written letters, friends told me I should write a book.
How do you write a book? All the thoughts, experiences,
events and pictures crammed into my head – and no
talent to express them clearly so that others might
share them and feel the same emotion as I felt it.

Immediately after enrolling in the Famous Writers
School my mind was alive with topics to write about.
Even in church I couldn't concentrate because each new
thought expressed by the minister would bring to my
mind another gem of information to add to my growing
list of topics. I could hardly wait to begin.

Beginning brought a whole new set of problems. As
I worked on the assignments I began to feel stale and to
feel that my original thought was really useless after
all. I wondered if this would always be true or would I
eventually be able to sustain a freshness in this original thought even after numerous rewritings. I even

resented the paperback books supplied with the course. How could I be expected to write like that?

Studying writing has brought a new awareness and interest of things around me. Now, instead of just seeing the face of a new acquaintance or an old friend, I mentally try to discover words to describe that face, to describe his mannerisms so that if someone were to read my description he would have an accurate mental picture of that person.

Childhood is such a fleeting period of life and with my four children growing up all too quickly I'd like to write a collection of their experiences and the few clever things they've said. If this collection is well written, reading these vignettes would recall to mind the exact incident and accompanying emotion just as seeing an old photo conjures up memories.

I do not delude myself into thinking that I have a message for the world, I only wish I did. I do think that I've had experiences, sad, happy and exciting that may be of interest to someone if I can learn to write them in a clear and expressive manner.

The inner self is our wants, wishes, fears, secrets, sorrows, and heartfelt thoughts. In Mom's letters to me and perhaps in the prior passage, she exposed her inner self: her fear of whether her writing would be of value, her want of that value, and her inner-self wish to be a successful writer. Fear itself often keeps the inner self secret. My mom rarely exposed her heartfelt wants and wishes, and she had only a small amount of allowance for sorrows and fears—hers or those of others. Accepting or displaying vulnerability was not in her outer-self bailiwick.

When writing personal letters, Mom was less guarded than when writing her life stories for coursework. "Once it's written, it's there forever" was her inner-self fear. Exposing her secrets, wishes, wants, and maybe even her shames required a vulnerability that she had squelched long ago. It was replaced by an unyielding self-protection, without which she might have been more viciously damaged early in her life. Her written stories were good, but the spoken tales had more authentic voice, more grit.

She once said to me, "If you'd write like you talk, it would be better." Now that I've read her cherished collection of story writings, I think this was the pot calling the kettle black.

JUNE'S AUNT LYDA

In 2013, a movie was released called *The Homesman*, starring Hilary Swank and Tommy Lee Jones. The release was not a huge marketing blowout, but more a soft release, and only shown in one of the artsy theaters in my area. I was aware of it because of two factors. One: the story takes place in the late 1800s and is specific to the pioneers settling the west and more specifically to the effect such life struggles had on women. Two: I love Tommy Lee Jones! I think I've seen every movie he's ever made, beginning with *The Betsy* in the late 1970s. *Coal Miner's Daughter* ranks way up there as an all-time favorite, and *Lonesome Dove* and *Blue Sky* ... well, he's just my kind of guy. I'm drawn to strong, rugged, manly-men;

I never want a man prettier than I am. And I'm drawn to a sense of humor and smarts. Of course, my perception is only that of a fan, but I think he's smart; he did attend Yale University. He's also a fantastic actor.

As the movie begins, the audience is aware of the sparse prospects for husbands for the pioneer women and soon thereafter aware of the isolationism young women and wives suffered. The bulk of the story depicts the lead characters transporting three young wives back east to Ohio so their mental illnesses, developed from a life of depravity, loneliness, and sorrow, could be treated. Of most importance to me, the movie reflected the rural life of the westward pioneers and perhaps offered a glimpse into Fannie's younger life.

One scene I barely recall for its dialogue and purpose because my eyes and mind were so fixated on the setting. There was a home, a residence with only a front façade. There were no sides to the structure; it wasn't even a structure, just the front, which was constructed with layers of sod. The entire body of the home was a hole dug out in the side of a hill. I knew from storytelling that Fannie had lived in a similar dwelling.

Barbara June barely knew her maternal relatives. While she was born and raised in Southern California, her extended family lived in Oklahoma. A couple of photos prove a visitation when she was about five years old, but she had little memory of the trip. The second trip, a hitchhiking excursion, took place when she was thirteen. Her knowledge of Fannie's five sisters and four living brothers came from storytelling and letters. Her aunts Maggie and Jessie appeared to be most favorable in their relationship with Fannie.

They were five and seven years younger than my grandmother. Lyda was the last-born girl of the clan. Another son was born after her, but I have the distinct impression Lyda was considered the baby of the family. She also grew to be the most petite of the sisters. I was told she married well, a lawyer, if memory serves.

The older children were undoubtedly Lyda's caregivers. By the time Lyda was born, their mother, Rosa, had spent seventeen years birthing a baby approximately every eighteen months. Rosa was probably filled to the brim in birthing, nursing, and caring for children. She even suffered a breakdown similar to those reflected in the movie *The Homesman*. Fannie was nine when Lyda was born—not grouped with the older ones and certainly no longer a baby. Perhaps she was charged with caring for Maggie and Jessie, and their bond developed.

Great Aunt Lyda wrote of their early life. She quoted from a popular television series from the 1970s called *The Waltons* in prefacing her writing: "When asked by his publisher, 'Do you want me to check it over and correct it?' John Boy Walton replied, 'I do not. I want my book to sound like me.'" John Boy's comment applies to my story, too. I can relate. However, her story is long and occasionally repetitive, so I've taken liberties. She wrote of their patriarch, Victor, with great admiration and detail. Credit to their mother, Rosa, was leveraged at perhaps ten percent. Victor died at thirty-eight years of age, leaving Rosa with eleven children—the youngest was just eleven days old. Give me a break! *There's* a story!

Lyda's Story

The 1880s were not prosperous years for the people of southern Kansas. The crops were only fair and the economics of the time left much be desired.

Victor Waterbury, my father, owned a small farm and the possibility of saving enough money to buy one that was larger was slight. His family was out-growing his farm. For over two centuries, families of America had traveled west when they wanted more room. Land was available in Eastern Colorado. All that was necessary was to find a quarter section (160 acres) that had not been claimed, stake your claim, make some improvements, live on it for a while and it was yours. After much deliberation, the decision was made; they would go to Colorado.

Careful planning was required to such an expedition. It was a 300 miles journey to a new permanent home. They knew that much would have to be taken with them since they were going to an area where settlements were small and far apart. Travel would be by covered wagon with an additional wagon to carry a plow and other farming tools, a crate of chickens and a water barrel. The livestock could drink from ponds and streams along the way, but it was necessary to have a barrel for drinking water and for cooking. The wagons also contained a cook stove, dishes, pans, bedding and all of their clothes and a supply of groceries. They had the little hand-powered grist mill and cans of ground grain which was a major part of their food. One of the wagons also served as a living room and a place to sleep. One wagon was pulled with horses and the other by oxen. The cattle were herded by Hattie who was seven, and Carl who was five.

When they found good grass along the trails they would stop and let the livestock graze. At best, progress was slow. Ten miles was a good day's travel. Every day consisted of building a fire, milking the cows and cooking breakfast, which was mostly graham mush made from the ground wheat and occasionally biscuits and eggs, if the hens cooperated, and of course, milk.

As they traveled westward, the land was so level they could see for miles in every direction and the little towns became farther apart.

Finally the day arrived when they stopped the wagons on what appeared to be a good piece of land just a few miles west of the Kansas-Colorado line and a few miles north of the Oklahoma border, near the Cimarron River.

For three years they lived in Colorado. Father provided a one room sod house which was made by digging a cellar-like room about three to four feet deep. Around this, blocks of sod were stacked, much like bricks in a wall. Spaces were left for the door and a few windows. Sisters Hattie and Maggie remembered they had to go up a ladder to get to the outside. The roof was constructed of poles covered with thatching obtained from watergrass or cattails, found in the natural surrounding area.

Obtaining water was one of the perpetual chores. There were no wells nearby. Every third day, Mother would hitch a team to the wagon containing the empty barrels. She and the three smaller children, with Hattie and Carl on horses, would drive the cattle three miles to the river. The animals could graze along the way and drink their fill at the river while the barrels were being filled. Mother would stand in the water with a bucket she'd fill and hand to Hattie and Carl to carry and pour into the barrels. Once the barrels were filled, they'd pick up wood and dead tree limbs to be hauled back to the home.

There were no fences so Father made a corral to hold the livestock at night. When the fence was complete, Father started building a barn to house the horses during the winter storms. Two rows of poles, arranged about eighteen inches apart, were covered on the inside with woven wire, then filled with hay and packed down by trampling. The woven wire was necessary to prevent the animals from eating the walls. The roof of the A-frame barn was made of poles covered with hay and thatch.

The second summer was a pleasant one. The rains came frequently and their garden and small field of corn grew nicely. Soon they would have sweet corn

*to partner with some of the garden vegetables. Then
disaster occurred. They awakened one morning to
find a herd of range cattle (belonging to others) had
broken down the fence and everything had been eaten
or trampled to the ground. This was the price paid for
trying to settle land which was largely controlled by
the established cattlemen who contended that all land
was common property and no fences were to be built.
Once, when Father was working on his fences, two "free
range" horsemen rode up and made demands that he
should leave the country. Father stood his ground and
finally they pulled their guns and started firing all too
near his feet for comfort.*

*One winter evening when Father was doing his
chores in the barn a snow storm struck. When he
had finished, he took the lantern and started for the
house about fifty yards due north. The storm was so
intense he could not see the light in the window. He
headed toward what he thought was the right course,
when suddenly he stumbled over a wagon seat that
he remembered was setting just east of the house. He
turned to the left and found the house only a few steps
away. Had he missed the wagon seat he would have
perished in the storm, most likely.*

This describes the three years encompassing Fannie's birth,
as she was born during this westward expedition. Historians
have recorded the winter of 1888–1889 to be the worst winter

on record, which probably explains the families' failure in the venture. Her father needed to make trips to Springfield, Lamar, or Trinidad, Colorado, or Liberal, Kansas, to source corn, wheat, and coal. These trips could take five to ten days. Of course, during those trips, Rosa was left at home, caring for five children under the age of seven and tending the livestock. Such reflects a far less glamorized, real-life version of *"Little House on the Prairie"*

HER MOTHER

Barbara wrote of her mother using Fannie's middle name, Phoebe, and Will for her father's name. She wrote the story when she was in her mid-forties. Barbara married at nineteen and moved an hour or two away, ending the opportunity for her to have close physical proximity to her mother. In those days, without possession of a car, they couldn't visit very often. Even after Barbara's first divorce, visitation was minimal. She was living in the San Diego area, and Fannie was in Pomona. Without vehicle transportation, the distance might as well have been halfway across the county.

The presence (or intrusion) of a stepfather was unwelcomed by her as a teenager, while it was surely the best benefit for Fannie. Idean had to move out for the sake of *appearances*. My mother admitted to not being very nice to Fannie and Henry. A surly teenager in the mid-1940s was nothing compared to a rebellious teen in 2020, but still, she confessed to having her moments. Like all late-teens, she was distancing herself emotionally and then geographically with her first marriage. The moments passed, evidenced by her inscription on the graduation photo she gifted to Fannie and

Henry: *To Mom & Henry. A swell pair of parents. Love to you both, June.* Swell. A great word for the times.

Barbara had a bit of guilt later in life for not having shown sufficient appreciation or gratitude to Fannie. All her mother's sacrifices and efforts to protect, provide, and support the two of them had been extreme. Barbara regretted feeling embarrassed of her mother when she was younger. She never, ever spoke an unkind word about her mother to us.

Fannie's resilience and self-reliance during Mom's childhood were solid, and Mom modeled the same in her own young adulthood. Barbara accepted total responsibility to handle decisions and difficulties by herself. She didn't expect or request assistance from Fannie.

Her path of getting married and beginning life as an adult, wife, and mother was the prescribed norm in the late 1940s. All of her friends had followed that path a year or two earlier. She had feelings of wanting better and being better than the life she was provided, so she married. When she abandoned that plan, she accepted being alone with two small children, solving her own problems and challenges. As the years passed, her appreciation stockpiled for her mother's efforts to protect and provide. Mom's story documents her gratefulness.

Phoebe

After she died, a friend said, "Phoebe could always make something out of nothing." Phoebe spent most of her life making something out of nothing but always with a great big laugh.

She met and married Will, a poor farm hand, and bore two sons and a daughter. They lived on a farm during those early years, Will working as a hired hand and Phoebe cooking on a wood stove for twenty-five farm hands. She was energetic and she moved at a fast pace. She especially enjoyed laughing and joking with the farm crew. Eventually Phoebe and her family left the farm and moved to Los Angeles. Will began to drink heavily and Phoebe took a job as a presser in a garment factory to support the family. Finding solutions to problems within her control was easy for Phoebe, but she had no solution for her alcoholic husband but to take one day at a time.

Phoebe's ability to laugh under the most adverse conditions was put to the test many times during the next few years. When Will would get drunk and begin to rant and rave in the middle of the night, Phoebe would quietly gather up her daughter who was ten, and they would sneak out of the shabby apartment and down the back stairs of the building and quickly run down the alley before Will could realize they were gone. Phoebe had nobody to help her, so she would just stay away from the apartment until she was certain that Will had passed out. During one of these nighttime treks Phoebe and her daughter stopped at a little coffee shop to splurge on a cup of hot chocolate. It was about five in the morning, and the waiter, trying to be friendly, asked if they were on the way

to the Four Square Gospel Church to hear Aimee
Semple McPherson preach at one of her early morning services. Phoebe just laughed that big laugh and
winked at her daughter and then very elegantly said
they were just out for an early morning walk.

Christmas during those difficult years seemed
to bring Phoebe's talent for resourcefulness and
laughter to the surface. One Christmas during those
Great Depression years Phoebe knew there would be
no money for a Christmas tree. She went down to a
Christmas tree lot and asked the man in charge if she
could have some of the discarded branches strewn
all over the ground. After getting permission, Phoebe
gathered up as many branches as she could carry,
took them home and scrounged for an old piece of flat
lumber to use as a tree trunk and nailed the branches
to this board in the shape of a Christmas tree. It wasn't
beautiful, but with the bulbs and glittering tinsel, it was
a Christmas tree.

After Will died, Phoebe moved to a small town in
southern California feeling almost relieved that now she
might find her life a little more peaceful. Even though
she was growing older, her posture was still straight,
her step was still agile, her movements were quick and
that big laugh brought out the best in everybody. She
cleaned office buildings, she worked as a mother's
helper, and she took in washing but there was never
enough money. Phoebe was trying to figure out a way

that she could give her daughter a cedar chest as a high school graduation present. Graduation time was near, but there wasn't any money for a cedar chest. She went to a second-hand store and bought a rusty old trunk and then spent hours making quilted upholstery for that old trunk. That old rusty trunk became a beautiful gift.

Once all of Phoebe's children were grown and married she kept busy making quilts, knitting slippers and crocheting doilies and pot holders. Her one luxury was to take a trip on a bus. She enjoyed being with people and getting to know them for even a short time. She would talk with everyone near her and then take such delight in retelling her experiences numerous times.

Phoebe is gone now, but that big laugh still rings in the ears of all who knew her, and the fruits of her resourcefulness linger in countless homes.

I have a couple of Fannie's handmade doilies. I framed them against cherry-red velvet fabric. In general, I'm not a fan of antiques, or "old stuff" as my Mom would say. She used to say, "I lived with old stuff all my life. I don't want anything that looks old." We don't have any appreciation for antiques. But I'm glad I have those doilies and a few other keepsakes of my grandmother's.

When I first heard the story about the Christmas tree, told by my mom, I had nothing to say. I was dumbstruck. We always had a Christmas tree, even if for many years it was a Sears catalog, four-foot artificial tree. We always had presents, even if they included socks and underwear.

I can visualize a mother and a five-year-old little girl striding down the block on a mission to get the job done. I can see Fannie, swinging a hammer with the might of an old farm girl, building her makeshift Christmas tree. I'm aghast and impressed that Fannie did not feel any entitlement to a free or nickel-priced tree, nor did she even fathom the idea of taking the discarded branches without permission. Integrity. Too many people tell stories of pulling one over on someone, of pulling a fast one, of being pleased with themselves in conniving to get something for nothing. That's not how my mother was taught, and not how I was taught.

Escaping in the middle of the night was a repetitive occurrence. They often went to bed in their clothes so their escape was swift. Usually they went to a seedy all-night movie theater until morning arrived and they could return to their apartment. I'd have felt smothered by the required vigilance. Every evening, the anticipation of having to escape loomed over them. I'm not sure who was in more danger, Fannie or June. Given that June was in grade school and couldn't yet protect herself, finding a solution was left to Fannie. She chose flight versus fight.

When telling of these occurrences much later in life, Barbara relayed the events with an edge of humor, an edge of "Can you believe that?" She never saw herself as a victim. Ever.

I didn't know of Fannie's DIY skills early in my adult life. I knew of my mom's skills. They were on display all the time— chronic normal processes. I began to build things myself at age twenty-two. I wanted to build a stereo shelf unit. I planned it in my head and went to the lumber store. After telling the clerk the number of one-by-four, one-by-six, and one-by-two-inch boards I needed, cut in specific lengths, the guy looked at me with a slight scowl and asked, "What are you making?" Feeling his cynicism, I replied, "What does it matter?" Then I asked him in which aisle I could find a hammer and nails, which probably confirmed his skepticism. Didn't matter, it turned out just fine and served its purpose for sixteen years, first as a stereo and album shelf, and later, with some refurbishing, for my computer printer and binder storage. As years passed, purchasing more tools and gaining skills, I've built numerous items that have surprised my friends. I refer to Home Depot as my personal Disneyland. I'd learned by repetitive example from Mom. She'd learned from Fannie.

There is great joy is completing a project, the ability to say "Done!" My professional work is a treadmill of repetitive, never-ending tasks. DIY projects grant me completion. Even if it's easier to purchase ready-made items, I still seek the planning, building, or sewing.

At thirty-one, I was transferred back to Chicago and I didn't want to go. I'd used all my savings to purchase my first home, and by my own reckless spending, I was in significant credit card debt. With no savings left and monthly bills and mortgage payments due, I was a slave to the next paycheck. Any choice I had to not make the move was quashed by my own doing. I was mad at myself for spending beyond my income.

After accepting the relocation, I buckled down and removed all debt in the next two years, then paid cash for a car and new bedroom furniture, plus a couple other furnishings, and vowed to be more frugal. I decided to build and upholster a headboard. I was working in a wealthy area near Northwestern University and employed a number of students. Many came from a more privileged life. I relayed the plan to a small group of servers. One young student/waitress lifted her hand, and with her thumb and forefinger in an "L" shape, held it to her forehead and said "Loser." What? I was taken aback. This was a taste of snob, of elitist criticism. I could write it off to her youth, ignorance, and spoiled life and not let it affect me, but I never forgot it. I sold the headboard at a garage sale fifteen years later to a very grateful young woman, complete with the coordinating duvet cover I'd sewn.

My mom didn't care for knick-knacks, tchotchkes, small figurines, or anything of the sort. "Just clutter to collect dust," she'd say. As the years passed, her kids would gift her various small décor items, and she did like those, if only in honor of the giver. When she moved to a brand-new, smaller home at the age of seventy-nine, I assisted in unpacking box after box of things she had kept. She was not a pack rat, far from it, but she struggled to dispose of most any gift or no-longer-used household item that "I may use someday, or *someone* may have use for it."

Her two-car garage was more than half-filled with boxes stacked four feet tall. By this time, I fully owned her get-out-of-my-way, get-it-done methods, so I brought out the kitchen stool so she could sit while I barreled through the work. By now, she'd tagged me as a "whirling dervish of productivity." Carefully, with knowledge of which of my siblings had gifted which items, we purged useless or broken items and chose where to display the balance. Nearing the bottom of one box, I picked up a two-inch ceramic figurine of a pink swan with a white rose and tiny golden trim. The body of the swan is a cavity with an opening at the top, but for the life of me, I don't know what would go in there. This item was contrary to anything my mother would choose, or like. It's a dime-store item, with a "Japan" stamp on the bottom. I picked it up, held it up for her to see, and with exasperation in my tone, asked, "Why are you keeping this?" She let out a little sigh and replied, "My mother gave that to me."

Well! How about that!? That thing had been carted around in some box, in and out of the country, back and forth across the country, with every move we'd made. Yet, I'd never seen it before this day. In all the years past, she hadn't touted the item as something special to her. The box it was in was full of forgotten items, unused for a good number of years. She kept it for the same reason I keep her letters. Just so I have them. I chose a place for honorable display, on a shelf in my mom's home office space next to a small, pink-and-white ceramic picture frame containing a portrait of Fannie.

When Fannie died, Mom had possession of her wedding rings. The band is simple ten-carat gold, and the accompanying ring is also ten-carat with an emerald-cut, pale-green piece of glass. Today, it would be called a manufactured gem. When I visited her, I'd always look at those rings. I loved that they fit me and were clearly too big for my mom or my sisters. Upon the occasion of my fortieth birthday, Mom asked what I wanted for a gift. Gift giving was not extravagant in our family, and wants were always less important than needs, so I knew she was inquiring about a need. I went out on a limb and asked her if I could have those rings, if not today, then in the future. She replied, "What rings?!" oblivious to my request. Then she mailed me one of the rings. I feared I'd overstepped in asking. When I tried to apologize, again she had no idea what I meant. She said, "Oh, you know I don't care about such things. Of course, you can have them. I just didn't realize you wanted them both."

I had never really known my grandmother, but my love for my mother was more than enough for transference to Fannie. Barbara was not sentimental, at all. She was not sappy about anything. No, I think I have enough of that trait for the both of us, a clear example of nature versus nurture.

MY DAUGHTER WILL DO THAT

As unstable, impoverished, and precarious as her childhood was, it was what she knew. It was her normal. Yet, this particular story from my mom's life had a unique distinction to her and therefore to me. She was proud of this experience. Proud of the fearlessness her mother projected and, by extension, she projected. When she relayed this incredulous event to friends, their response was one of wide-eyed awe. They just couldn't believe such an experience happened. She enjoyed their response, and it granted her a bit of sassiness in the telling.

Mom had written about it time and time again, sometimes in outline form and sometimes in essay form. Much later in her life, she had retold the story to a social group of women from her church. An acquaintance within the group was so taken by the story she asked my mother if she could write it. Although my mother had written the story multiple times herself and had often communicated her plans to write a book, she made no reference to her own work this time. Instead she replied, "No, my daughter is going to do that."

With her expectations in mind, fully embracing my responsibility to do justice in the telling, I've composed her written works as well as my memory of her spoken accounts. The lessons to be learned from this event are the sheer power of determination, the grace found in the kindness of strangers, and the safety that can be felt under the protection of a mother.

When June was thirteen years old, her mother decided they would travel from Los Angeles to Enid, Oklahoma, to visit Fannie's mother and sisters for Christmas. A vacation. Years later, she looked back on the excursion as perhaps her mother's attempt to leave her father, to leave the marriage.

They packed one cardboard suitcase with the few clothes they owned and carried their Southern California cloth coats and cotton gloves. They had expected to ride with someone they knew, sharing gas expenses along the way. Unfortunately, their ride didn't show up on the appointed day, or the next. Fannie was a "can-do" gal. She'd made her decision to make the trip, and they were going. They'd hitchhike. Hitchhiking was a fairly common method of transportation, so June wasn't scared.

They took a streetcar into Los Angeles, getting off at the General Hospital. From there they'd hitchhiked to Puente, where June's brother lived, to pick up what little bit of money he might provide, then they hitchhiked into Pomona, planning to get an early start the next morning.

Oklahoma by Christmas

Everyone must have thought we were nuts, but it seemed exciting and not too unusual to me.

My mother and I lived in a run-down sector of east, Los Angeles. It was during those uneasy days between the Depression and the War when most people had little money, but we had even less.

It was nearing Christmas and Mother wanted to spend the holidays with Grandma and all the other relatives in Oklahoma, but bus tickets were too expensive. She made her decision, and we were going. If we were careful, we would have enough money for meals during the trip, and hitchhiking was free so we were on our way.

At the beginning it was fun. We got rides quickly, and with my mother's skill in engaging with strangers and bringing humor to everything, the people were friendly and everybody laughed a lot. We had one cardboard suitcase and we carried lightweight coats over our arms. The further east we went, the colder it became.

We hopped a ride with a group of three people; two men and a woman. They must have been young, but at my tender age of thirteen they seemed old. All were fair complexioned with non-descript faces, and the woman had dark hair. She had just married the driver of the car, but she was necking with the other man. All were drinking heavily, and the bridegroom was driving much too fast: ninety miles per hour. It was a lonely road, and I knew that Fannie was scared just as much as I was, so she asked them to stop and let us out. The woman finally talked them into stopping.

They all had another drink, and then the men went behind the cactus to go to the bathroom and the woman slipped behind the steering wheel, so she could drive. We crossed the California border three times that day. We were so glad to be out of that car but yet felt discouraged because we had backtracked all day. A whole day wasted and we were so short of time, as we wanted to be in Oklahoma by Christmas day. The three people had promised to take us further, but we had changed our mind. Fannie did not want to get back in that car again. She really knew how to handle the drunks!

Another ride was a grey haired man with two daughters. Their mother had just died, and one daughter was pregnant. They were evidently pretty wealthy because they were well dressed and had a large black touring car and insisted on paying for our meals when we stopped for dinner. I almost hated to leave their car – it had a certain security and yet I was glad to get away from the sadness. The pregnant daughter had to take Bromo-seltzer for her upset stomach. They were very kind to us.

Then a ride came from a hay truck driver over the treacherous mountains in Arizona. He was a heavy set man with dark curly hair, and he needed a shave, but he was very jolly. The truck was perched on the edge of the narrow mountain road near Gallup, New Mexico. Fannie and I sat inside the truck cab while the driver checked his load height for clearance through a low mountain tunnel. The load of hay would make it through, but our cardboard suitcase would have to come down. I was certain that if I moved even a toe, the truck would roll backwards, into the deep canyon. By this time, I just bit off the last traces of fingernails.

All of the characters we met were kind and considerate of Fannie, and she always joked with them, laughing her big old laugh. Now, we were heading into a snow storm and it was Christmas Eve.

Each day we had changed our clothes in a gas station restroom because so far we had been lucky enough to catch rides with people who traveled through the night. It was snowing and my legs were freezing as we walked along the New Mexico highway with scarcely a car in sight. I had a pair of slacks in the suitcase, but in my typical rebellious manner I had chosen to wear a skirt and blouse that day.

Out of nowhere a snowball splattered to the pavement at our feet. We turned to look and saw a group of four or five boys standing behind a snow bank in front of a brown rustic log-cabin-type building. The boys were scooping up handfuls of snow and packing them together to make snowballs.

Mother, trying to look stern, yelled to the boys, "Did

you throw that snowball at me?" I wanted to ignore the incident and just keep on walking. These boys weren't much older than I, perhaps fourteen or fifteen, and I wasn't ready to admit an interest in boys, so I acted completely uninterested.

The next thing I knew, Mother scooped up a handful of snow, packed it into a snowball, and heaved it at the group. It was a perfect shot. The boys stood in stunned silence for a moment then they began to shout and holler and the snowballs flew back and forth. I thought I would die of embarrassment. My mother, acting like a little kid, throwing snowballs at a bunch of boys and worst of all, she was enjoying it.

The fight was soon over and the laughing had almost stopped, when one boy said, "What are you guys doing out here?"

"We're heading for Oklahoma to spend Christmas, but there're not many cars on the road today," Fannie replied.

"You hitchhiking?" said one of the boys in disbelief. My cheeks burned with embarrassment at the revelation. I didn't think it was any of their business.

The group of boys lived at a Civilian Conservation Camp, better known as CC Camp, an organization formed during Franklin D. Roosevelt's time to maintain our national parks and at times to act as an interim home for problem boys. One of the boys ran into the camp office and came back out in a few minutes with the camp director, a tall, rugged man with black hair and eyes to match.

"My boys tell me you're hitchhiking and having a little trouble getting a ride. Listen, we're expecting our milk delivery truck to come through here in a couple of hours, and I'm sure that Sam would be glad to take you as far as Albuquerque. That is, unless you'd rather stay out here and try to catch a ride."

Mother glanced down the deserted road and said, "We'll take you up on that."

"Good," said the man, "why don't you come on in the dining hall and get warm and you can have supper with us before Sam gets here. I think the boys would like that."

As we stepped into the dining hall, the warm, spicy smell of turkey and dressing greeted us. It was a big square room with open rafters, knotty pine walls, and long varnished tables with attached benches already set for supper. In the middle of the room was an immense wood-burning pot-bellied stove that heated the entire room. As we ate our supper and I listened to my mother laugh and joke with the boys, I had a mixture of feelings. I was still embarrassed with my mother because of the snowball fight and I was ashamed that the boys knew about the hitchhiking, but mixed with these feelings was secret smugness. This woman, whom all the boys seemed to like, was my mother. She was in control, in-charge, and showed no fear. Therefore, I didn't either.

Not long after supper Sam arrived with his milk truck at the back entrance of the dining room. The camp director had gone out to meet Sam and we could see through the frosty dining room windows that he was talking to Sam about us. Sam was a short man with powerful shoulders and a baby-smooth complexion. He wore a hunting cap with the ear flaps up so that he looked like a puppy dog with floppy ears. Sam was nodding his head up and down then the camp director came back into the dining room to tell us we had a ride to Albuquerque.

Sam was a slight but strong man in his early thirties who delivered milk to the CC Camps in New Mexico. His one-hundred-and-fifty-mile milk route began and ended in Albuquerque. Because of the storm, Sam and his helper Vic were running late on their route. Vic was a high school boy who helped Sam during Christmas vacation. Vic was a little shy, didn't talk much, and he felt a little uncomfortable with Mother and me in the truck.

Sam lifted the heavy milk crates as if they were as light as eggs and pushed them to the back of the panel truck to make room for my mother and me to sit on an old discarded car seat that he squeezed behind the front seats. The cotton padding was showing through and a few of the springs were broken, but it was quite comfortable. As we left, my mother waved and shouted goodbye to the boys, but I just looked the other way.

Sam made one more milk delivery before he headed

for home in Albuquerque. He and my mother did a lot of talking and laughing. She told him about California and he told her about his wife and two children who were expecting him home that night so he could attend the church Christmas program. He wasn't going to be home in time.

The big snowflakes were coming down faster now. Sam hunched forward, straining to see the narrow road as it wound through the heavily wooded area. Occasionally he would wipe the steam from the windshield with his gloved hand.

"Gosh darn it," said Sam. "I was sure hoping to get through with these milk deliveries before this storm got too bad, but I don't know if we're gonna make it or not."

Fannie leaned forward from the makeshift back seat and said, "This ain't bad, Sam." She gave him a knowing wink with a slight jerk of her head towards me sitting beside her, and he understood. "Once when I was a young girl I had to wade through snow clear up to my waist and walk five miles to school."

"You must have been just tall enough to reach a grasshopper's eyeballs then, 'cause I ain't never seen snow that deep around here," said Sam.

"Lordy, that was long before you were even born! I'm old enough to be your mother."

"You sure don't look it." Sam reached up and wiped the steam off the windshield again, and added, "I–I didn't mean we weren't really gonna make it to

Albuquerque, I just meant that it's gonna take a little longer than I thought." He glanced in the rear view mirror and gave a quick wink to Fannie, as if to say, "Does that make it better?"

I was huddled close to my mother and shivering, more from nervousness than from the cold. I had seen the exchange of winks between Fannie and Sam and knew it was an attempt to keep me from being frightened by the snowstorm and the slippery roads. Sam, trying to divert attention from the storm, said, "Hey, Vic, got any more of those gumdrops?"

Vic leaned down and felt around under the seat and came up with a paper bag that was soft and crumpled from being opened and closed a lot. Vic offered the sack to my Mother and she reached in and took a gum drop.

"Thank you," said Mother. She chuckled as she said, "I just got the last gum drop out of my upper plate."

Vic offered the sack to me, but I merely shook my head. Vic offered the sack to Sam. He took off one glove with his teeth and reach into the sack for a gum drop.

"Don't know what there is about gumdrops, but I sure do like 'em. I was going to take this sack to my kids, but I guess maybe they won't know the difference. They shouldn't eat so much candy anyway. Most kids eat too much candy nowadays."

Vic looked at the nearly empty sack, grinned, and said quietly, "How come you eat so much candy, Sam?"

"Shut up, boy, that's different." Sam laughed at himself.

"You two warm enough back there?" Sam asked. Sam had turned the heater on high since Mother and I weren't dressed for cold winter weather with just light-weight coats and thin gloves. Sam and Vic had unbut-toned their heavy wool Mackinaws and pushed them back from round their necks.

"We're fine," Mother replied.

We rode on in silence for a little while watching the snow surround us.

"We Three Kings of Orient Are," sang Sam. "You know I like that song. My kids were supposed to sing it in the Christmas play at school tonight. Boy is my old lady gonna be mad because I missed it. I always complained that I had to, but I'm kinda sorry that I'm missing it too." Sam wiped the steam again from the windshield. The snow was falling faster and the wind was howling. The narrow road was almost invisible. Sam glanced at Mother in the rear view mirror and said, "Beats me why anyone would ever want to leave California. If I ever get out of this part of the country, I'm never coming back. Any jobs in California?"

"Not many," Fannie replied. "Lotsa people still working for the Works Progress Administration."

The road was rougher now, and Sam was care-fully trying to steer the old panel truck between ruts of ice. The old truck rattled along, and the milk bottles clattered against the metal bands of the wooden crates. Suddenly the truck hit a mound of ice, bounced up, and then slid off into a rut with a terrible scraping noise. Mother and I hit our heads on the ceiling of the truck.

"Whoa there," hollered Sam, as if he was reining in a team of horses.

Sam pulled off to the side of the road, buttoned up his Mackinaw, and pulled the earflaps down on his cap. He took a flashlight from the dashboard and got out of the truck. He walked around the vehicle, kneeling down and checking the tires and then the underside of the truck. When he opened the door and quickly got back inside, he said, "Brrrr, it's cold out there." He was beating his hands together to brush the snow off his gloves. "Looks like we've got a problem, Vic. I think maybe the gas tank has sprung a leak."

Sam knew the route well, even in the blinding storm. We made our way to a garage and waited while the leak could be welded. It was bitterly cold, and we stood huddled around a wood stove in one corner of the garage.

Once back in the truck, Sam asked, "How far did you say you were going?"

"We wanted to get to Enid, Oklahoma, by tomorrow. I figure if we can get a ride out of Albuquerque tonight, we should be able to make it," replied mother.

"Gee, I dunno, that's over five hundred miles from Albuquerque and this storm doesn't look like it's going to let up."

"We'll make it," Mother said. Sam didn't know that
we didn't have enough money for a hotel room so we
had to find a ride. We rode on in silence until we reached
Albuquerque. It was eight o'clock in the evening and the
downtown streets were snow covered. Sam was driving
very carefully and very slowly.

"I have one more stop to make here in town and
then I'll take you to the highway at the edge of town.
I wish I was going a little further. But ...," his voice
trailed off.

"That's okay, Sam, we're just lucky we got a ride
this far with you," Mother replied.

Sam drove a few more blocks and then pulled the
truck up in front of a small hotel and stopped. He
hopped out of the truck and called, "You wait here a
minute. I'll be right back."

A few minutes later, Sam came out of the hotel
and got into the truck. "Now look, I don't want any
argument from you. You just can't take off out of town
tonight. They've got an empty room at this hotel, so
you just stay put for tonight and then maybe tomorrow
the weather will be better and you can go on."

"Look Sam," my mother protested, "we just don't
have enough—"

Sam was firm, "Just hand me your suitcase and go
in the hotel. I gotta get home."

Sam carried our suitcase into the tiny lobby and set
it down. He shook hands with Mother and said, "Now

you just be careful who you ride with, and ... I hope you have a merry Christmas."

"You too, Sam. Thanks for the ride."

Sam hurriedly left the hotel. At the time, I thought he'd been glad to get rid of us. Mother walked up to the hotel desk and asked about a room. The desk clerk had Mother sign her name on a card and handed her the room key.

"How much is it?" asked Mother.

"It's all been taken care of ma'am," he replied.

It was still snowing when we woke up the next morning. I remember feeling a little sad, but Mother and I exchanged our small presents, long since forgotten, packed in our suitcase. I received only one gift, a box of handkerchiefs, and I gave only one gift, a homemade lapel pin with "Mother" written in alphabet macaroni.

We got a ride to a little country store about five miles outside of town and bought some milk and cookies. We stood out in the snow trying to get a ride and finally the store owner pleaded with us to go back to town and wait until the storm was over. We could never make it to Grandma's by Christmas anyway. I know that was a terrible disappointment to my mother. We took the storekeeper's advice and got a ride back to Albuquerque and back to the same hotel.

We spent Christmas Day walking the streets of Albuquerque and looking in the shop windows, stopping in a little café, and having a fried egg and cheese sandwich for Christmas dinner. We wanted to go to a movie but knew even the nickel was too much to spend. We went back to our hotel room and back to bed.

The next day was bright and sunny. When we had difficulty getting a ride, Mother said, "If we don't get a ride today, we're going to have to jump that freight train," as she pointed to a train on our left, on the horizon.

I may have been nervous before, or anxious, or even frightened, but this comment scared the soup out of me!

Luckily, we got a ride with some college students, returning to Florida, and a number of other rides for shorter stretches of road, as we got closer to Enid. We finally ended up in a drugstore where my mother telephoned one of her sisters, and they came to get us. I'm sure we were a bedraggled looking sight, and I know they were shocked at our adventure. Fannie would have never told them in advance, but now that it was over she could safely relay the events to them. None of my aunts and uncles would ever be in a position to have to hitchhike.

I loved the farms and loved being with family in clean farmhouses. One aunt baked and sold bread. The delicious aroma was more than I could take. I loved the fresh crusty heel when it was still hot and dripping with melted butter. I helped my aunt make her deliveries in a wagon through the town.

We stayed in Oklahoma long enough for the decision to be made to enroll me in school. I didn't question

the decision; the whole trip was just a great big adven-
ture. One day the school bus got stuck in the snow. I
thought it was hilarious. I walked two miles in the snow
with thin Jodhpur boots (picked up at the Salvation
Army – I thought they were so stylish) to get my uncle
to come with the tractor and help pull the bus out of the
ditch. Like a nut, I walked the two miles back to the bus,
and my aunt had to take me to some farmhouse and
they put my feet in cold water. They must have thought,
"That dumb city kid from California."

I have a lapel pin that was in a box of letters and keepsakes Mom saved for me. But it isn't the one my mother made for Fannie; it is one I made for my mother. It was a craft project when I was in a Brownie troupe at seven years of age. I don't know if alphabet macaroni was invented by 1940. I'm skeptical that small presents were packed in their suitcase. Maybe, maybe not. Perhaps Barbara was choosing to present some image of normalcy, or to disguise their "have-not" life with the mention of gifts.

Eventually, the time came for June and Fannie to go home to California. I doubt my mother wanted to go back. She was in school and surrounded by extended family, and the omnipresent tension of her father's presence was removed. But they helped with work to earn enough money to buy bus tickets home. Isn't it funny my mom never wrote nor told a story about the bus ride home? I guess it was uneventful.

Our family visited Enid, Oklahoma, again when we were traveling across the country for one of our many family moves. Mom wanted some connection with the people belonging to Fannie. We visited Mom's Aunt Jessie, who was seven years younger than Fannie. The house was white but weathered and old, on a residential street with other houses all looking the same age and condition. We all walked through a front living room that was dark, as the sun was setting at the back of the house. Aunt Jessie led us through a doorway and entered the bright kitchen, with full sunporch-style windows at the back.

Jessie was not a delicate woman; in fact, she had a large face with masculine features. But I remember her being open, broad, welcoming, and full of energy. Perhaps she and Fannie were alike in personality and temperament. She almost stomped through the house versus walked, taking large strides with a heavy placement of each step. She plopped down in a kitchen chair, threw one elbow onto the back of the chair, and crossed her legs, swinging her top leg up and down. We dutifully sat around Jessie's kitchen table. It was Formica-topped with metal trim around the edge, and the chairs were metal with shiny, yellow vinyl seats.

We met Jessie's daughter, Mom's cousin Sarah Rose, and her husband and their two teenaged daughters. Those blonde confident girls came right into Great Aunt Jessie's house like they owned the place. Opened the refrigerator and pulled out a couple bottles of Dr. Pepper, talking nonstop about their day's activities. This behavior didn't happen in my world. For one thing, we never had soda pop in the fridge. For another, we never would have been allowed to act so *familiar* in someone else's house. If this was what knowing your grandmother was about, then I missed out (on more than just soda pop).

JUST AN ORDINARY MOTHER

Mom rarely spoke tenderness, rarely openly acknowledged when something touched her heartstrings. She would never speak about having done something nice for someone, of having shown a gesture of kindness beyond common courtesy. She thought others who spoke of their "do-for-others" efforts were haughty and self-congratulatory. One time, in fourth grade, a school friend of mine was with us in the car and was bragging about her selflessness. I saw Mom grimace. Later, as she sucked air in through clenched teeth, she told me to never be like that. "You do nice things because it's the right thing to do, not to brag about it."

Tenderness was in her heart; she just didn't talk about it. I recall one evening in my early teens. Laundry day was Wednesday, if I remember correctly. We kids were responsible to strip our bed linens for washing before we left for school. Most times, she remade the beds before we came home. This particular Wednesday, when it was time to go to bed, I pulled back the covers and there was my bed, covered in lavender flowered sheets. Each bed in the house had new sheets with brightly colored flowers or stripes. Until then, all bedsheets had been plain old white. What a pretty surprise for us all. Decades later, I thought about her keeping this secret all evening long, through dinner, homework, and family television viewing, waiting for the moment when we'd all have this surprise.

The overwhelming majority of the stories Mom wrote were about *her* life. There are a couple of writings when we kids are mentioned, but we're not the main character. She made a conscious decision not to invade others' privacy, not to expose their lives, even her kids. I found this story about Paula within my mother's writings. I had never seen it before. Sharing it with my younger sister, Paula, over the phone, left us both in tears. Paula has never been much of a crier, at least not in front of others. Her comment was, "I never knew that Mom 'got me,'" that Mom understood her disposition. But now, with this story, she had confirmation. And another glimpse of the tenderness in our mother's heart.

Paula

Dear, sweet and loveable Paula. So quiet, so good and so undemanding. She lives with us almost like an angel – we only know she's with us because of her goodness. It seems she was never a baby–she just grew.

Yesterday the pedal of her second-hand bike, that has never worked properly, fell off and a part of the pedal was lost. Tonight as her father asked her if she had found the missing piece, she replied, "I already found it."

Dad asked where she had put it so he could fix the bike for her. "I already put it back on the bike."

No searching for glory, no begging for the bike to be fixed, no counsel, she just did the job that had to be done because it was there to do.

I'll miss the sweet hours at the dining room table playing Crazy Eight or Scotch Bridge with my six-year-old partner. Don't even know if she knows what she's doing, but she seems to play her cards with the wisdom and abandon of the older children. She wins too! But best of all, she doesn't cry when she loses.

I feel sad as I lift the sleeping Paula and encircle her arms around my neck and twist her legs around my waist to help ease her weight. She is almost too heavy for me to carry, and she is still such a little girl. She has never been small – even at birth she weighed over nine pounds with rolls of fat on her thighs. She is not fat now but big boned and sturdy. She is strong – can carry sacks of groceries from the car into the house, some of which seem to weigh almost as much as she does. It is apparently no effort for her to lift so much weight.

Paula loves her brother, Craig. Craig is four and a half years older than she and he returns this love, but not with quite the same deep feeling. I'm not saying they don't have their spats, and Paula is always ready to return blow for blow even if teasing, but during the first weeks of school and her first year of riding the school bus, Craig was her protector and big brother. After a few days, she became quite independent of Craig during the trip home. One day she got off the bus at the corner and slowly walked towards home. I was outside and noticed the concern on her face.

"Hi, Paula," I called.

"Hi," she said in such a hush tone. "Know what? Craig wasn't on the bus."

She was unmistakably afraid that something had happened to Craig. We walked on into the house and looked over her school papers and then I remembered that Craig had said he was to begin cello lessons that day and they were to be held after school. Such relief that Paula felt, when she knew that everything was alright.

One night as I was putting Paula to bed, she remarked, "I wonder what I will be when I grow up?"

I was hanging up a dress and putting away some clean folded socks and underwear, and I said, "I don't know, what do you want to be when you grow up?"

Paula gazed at the ceiling and very seriously said, "I guess I'll just be an ordinary mother."

What a great compliment to be just an ordinary mother.

Paula and I have talked about the inflection that would have been in Mom's voice when asking, "I don't know, what do you want to be when you grow up?" She would not have sounded gently thoughtful or tenderly inquisitive. That wasn't her. She was matter-of-fact, direct, and succinct. If Paula's response to be an "ordinary mother" brought Mom to a soft spot, it wouldn't have been perceptible. Unselfishly, such dialogues were not about her. Whether she knew it or not, she was teaching the lesson to do what you want, to make up your own mind, change your mind if you want to, and own your life.

Mom was always there when we arrived home from school. Always. Each of us would come in with our chatter and papers from the day's activity. Sometimes I think she offered only one ear, but one was better than none. I liked coming home to my mom and breaking the day's pattern, but I probably took her presence for granted.

On the last day of the school year, I recall walking into the house and Mom said, "Well, did you get promoted?"

How proud I felt to say, "Yes! I'm going to third grade next year." (We could earn a penny for every time we said "yes" versus "yeah." Paula earned the most pennies.)

Her question was a gift of support and pride in accomplishment. Oddly, today if I phrase the same question to an elementary school kid, they have no idea what I'm asking. How sad to miss out on a moment that brought me great joy.

Earlier in my life, right before our family moved to New Zealand on military orders, Fannie came to visit us for Christmas. I had a present under the tree "from Grandma." I opened the gift and was thrilled with a package of six pairs of Barbie-doll shoes. This was a great gift, and I expressed, "Thank you." Then Grandma said, "Oh, let me see that." I knew instantly. My mother had bought the Barbie shoes, wrapped them, and labeled the tag from her mother. She didn't tell her mother she had bought gifts for us kids "From Grandma." She just did it. I wasn't bothered that Mom had done that; in fact, it touched a soft spot in my eight-year-old heart. I knew it was a secret I wasn't supposed to know. She would have never told us Grandma didn't have enough money to offer gifts, but under no circumstance would she have wanted her mother to appear un-giving. Her tenderness was private.

III

On Alcohol

STRING UP THE NOOSE!

We adult kids had a good chuckle one day when my mom received a summons for jury duty. Somebody said, "You watch, it'll be a drunk-driving case."

Mom replied, "Yeah, and I'll say string up the noose!" It was. She was promptly released from service, early in the selection process.

She had her reasons, many reasons, alcohol never touched her lips. Except for one time. I recall at my older sister's wedding reception, she was urged to take a sip of champagne, and though she resisted, she did. I have to give her credit for not taking her usual unwavering, angry, adamant stance at that particular moment, potentially dampening the gaiety of the occasion. She went along with the chiding, took the sip, and made a face like she'd just bitten into a sour, rotted lime. That was the only time.

Her father was a drunk, the consummate be-all and end-all classic town drunk. Some of the repercussions of his drinking were written in her coursework; however, the most heinous were only told verbally, in short spurts of distaste when a specific incident brought the memories to the surface. The pain and sadness of these events were more than she could bear to write.

If she kept the worst only in her own memory, she could avoid the indignity of being a child victim and not suffer the shame she thought others might impose. *She* was not the drunk, and she would not expose herself to any shame because of the actions of her father.

As my mom aged into her late seventies, some of these old memories surfaced on occasion. When I visited her, if we weren't socializing with my siblings and we didn't have a DIY project on the visit agenda, we'd spend hours, even a full day, watching mindless old TV shows and movies, debating about what snack we could enjoy next. It was then that some of these stories were told.

When June was a young girl, she recalled the neighborhood boys, the "hooligans," on more than one occasion momentarily solving her father's drunkenness. They'd tie him to a tree on the sidewalk. Oh, he was still drunk, but at least he couldn't move, he couldn't do any harm—he was controlled. Can you imagine the degree of intoxication required to permit being tied up? She recalled walking up the steps to the door of their apartment house, intermittently glancing back at him tied up, and thinking "good." She was five years old.

She said to me, "Isn't that a horrible memory? That a little kid feels that way about their father?"

She spoke of another occasion, probably five to seven years later in her life, when she and her mother were attending church service. Her father came in the entrance and staggered up the middle aisle, yelling in his effort to find the two of them. He had no shirt on, nor shoes, and his belt was unbuckled with his fat belly hanging over the waistband of his pants. She had no words to describe her humiliation. She clenched her mouth and pursed her lips in a frown until the memory faded.

Once, almost as a slip-of-the-tongue, she told me of times she'd awakened in the middle of the night and had seen her father standing in her bedroom doorway, perhaps naked or at least barely clothed. When she told me about the countless times she and her mother would have to escape out a back door in the middle of the night, she'd said, "We'd heard him coming home."

I wondered what those sounds were. What did they hear? She used the phrase "ranting and raving." She and her mother would escape out the back door and spend a nickel at the all-night movie theater, so they could be safe and he could sleep it off. Safe from what? She never offered the details, and with both respect to her privacy and probably my own fear of the worst, I didn't ask.

In Mom's notes, she references the chronic evictions and moves in Los Angeles in her early childhood. Her father's failure to hold a job and his chronic drinking subjected his daughter (my mom!) to such appalling experiences.

Lived in cockroach ridden, bed bug infested, "light-housekeeping" rooms. Room was so small that I either slept alongside the bed on the floor on a palette (a new word that was unfamiliar to me but commonplace with my paternal renegade cousins) or slept with my head in the closet and my feet under the foot of the bed. Hallway so dark it was like eternal night. Only lived there a few short weeks until we moved to "permanent" place on Crocker Street.

Larger apartment – three rooms. I'm sure my mother must have hated living there since we had lived in houses as long as I could remember. My dad fought with the landlord.

Lived in lots of apartments in L.A. – moving many times, innumerable times. Another apartment was in a nicer section of town and I had one girl friend whose parents suddenly would not let her play with me. I wasn't even allowed to cross the threshold into their home. I didn't fully understand why at the time even though I knew it was because my father was an alcoholic. I couldn't understand, I wasn't an alcoholic!

Wall Street apartment: Horrible four-apartment building between two brick buildings. Across the street from a men's hotel. Kooky family downstairs: a mother, a father, and son and daughter. Daughter was a teenager and she and her mother loved to get all dressed up in full-skirted taffeta dresses with braiding all in loops around the bottom hem. They treasured those dresses so much that they kept their closet locked. My mother didn't especially like the family – the woman was too loose with her morals and all sorts of strange men coming and going at odd hours. The kids didn't go to school and couldn't read or write and the truant officer was always trying to get them in school. When the mother, who was expecting a baby (nobody knew whose baby), started in labor too soon, my mother went downstairs to help her and sent the daughter upstairs to our apartment. The baby was born dead, and I heard them talking about wrapping the baby in newspaper and putting it in the ice box until they could take it to the mortuary. My mother talked me out of some of my doll clothes to put on the baby to be buried in.

My paternal aunt – Religious one day and cussing everyone out the next. Lived with a current husband and a little boy but then her ex-husband lived there

too. I never could quite get all that straight. My cous-
ins always slept in their underclothes, and I know they
thought we were snobs because I put on pajamas at
night. This aunt would get mad at my mother for some
reason unknown to me, and I once heard her threaten
to throw Fannie "down the back stairs and break your
Goddamn back!" Terrified to go to school – afraid that I
wouldn't find mother alive when I came home.

Wholesale market for fruit and vegetables was
just a few blocks away. We used to make the rounds
daily in the early morning and go through the bins of
discarded produce (some with just a small spot but
they were not suitable for the retail stores) and carry
home all we could for our own use. I used to take only
fruit in my school lunch, with the bad spots cut out. I
was too proud to tell the real reason why I didn't bring
sandwiches: no bread. And the fruit had been free. I
can remember feeling almost wealthy when I had a new
metal lunch box with a thermos and hot vegetable soup
for lunch. In fact, I probably became quite snobbish over
the whole thing.

Most all of these stories were not shared with us kids when we
were younger. I know I reached the legal drinking age, not fully
knowing the extent of my mom's suffering as a result of alcohol.
But she did tell me one story when I was twelve years old. She was
about my age when her drunkard father chased her through the
streets of their neighborhood. Naked and scared, she had to run

into a church to seek safety. At the time, I had no information to connect this occurrence with alcohol, but I'll guarantee alcohol was at the root. While she had yet to relay the story of her hitchhiking trip to Oklahoma, as I put these two events in chronological order, it's probable the chase was the final straw that sparked Fannie's decision to leave.

While my mother never told of actual physical or sexual abuse, I've always suspected such. I mean, think about it: What purpose possibly could exist for a father, albeit a drunken father, to chase his naked, pubescent daughter through the streets? The chase itself was abuse! That night when she told me of this abuse, I was incapable of visualizing my mother as a thirteen-year-old girl. The story was a distant, disconnected event. However, I've thought about it often as an adult, with an adult's compassion and comprehension, and wonder how on earth she'd rebounded from the humiliation, the terror.

Yes, she had her reasons to be unyieldingly intolerant of any consumption of alcohol. Her suffering, more often than not, was alcohol induced. "String up the noose" was her expedient solution for crimes committed while intoxicated.

I'M NOT GONNA DO IT!

My mom's story titled "Summer Sunday" was written a number of times. Some accounts are long and detailed, others are pithy. All are written from slightly varying perspectives.

The longest version includes her instructor's feedback: "A good story that's strongest during the fight scenes, but you undercut some of it by the 'middle class' tone—we'll discuss this."

Whoa. I'll bet that stung. We *were* middle class, a dozen steps up from the economic class of her childhood. This comment may surely have rung in her ears as snobbery.

These life experiences were her truth. She wrote them from what she remembered. In this instance, the memory is that of a ten-year-old. Changing perspective from childhood memory to adult author assessing and relaying a story is arduous. She made alterations to lessen the filth and repugnancy, thereby unconsciously protecting herself from the risk of scorn. She would have vehemently labored over rewrites, seeking the perfect balance between her stubbornly ingrained childhood memories and compelling writing.

Summer Sunday

My father was an alcoholic. I don't drink and when people ask me why, I sometimes joke about growing up with an alcoholic. Then everybody laughs. Living with an alcoholic is not funny.

When I was ten years old, I remember a particular hot summer Sunday. The squeal of the police siren pierced through the noisy street sounds of southeast Los Angeles slum area. In a moment the patrol car skidded to a stop in front of a shabby, two-story, wood-frame apartment house for the third time that day. This time, Dad was going to jail.

Dad was a large, loose-featured man with a stomach that bulged over the top of his belt. The rear

*crotch of his wrinkled gray pants hung down almost
to his knees so that he looked like the rear view of an
elephant. Since early morning, he and the landlord had
been sitting on the wide front porch drinking cheap
port wine and arguing. Several times during the day
the arguments erupted into violent fights and twice the
neighbors called the police. When the police arrived,
announced by the wailing siren, they'd find Dad and
the landlord quietly sitting on the porch chairs, talking
congenially, with the bottle hidden behind a shrub.*

*On the occasion of the second visit, one of the
patrolmen warned, "If we get another call back to this
house you're both going to jail."*

*Dad and the landlord sat in their chairs and drank
wine all that day. Twice, they'd coerced me into going to
the liquor store to buy another bottle. They instructed
me to pick up any empty bottles in the surrounding
yards to redeem for deposit and bribed me with the
allowance to purchase a bag of peanuts for myself.*

*My mother spent the day in the apartment. She'd
spent the morning cleaning and spraying insecticides,
encouraging the cockroaches to go across the hall to
the next door apartment, at least for a day or two. The
rest of the day she worked in the apartment doing other
people's laundry.*

*Both men leaned their rickety wooden chairs
against the house, balancing on the two rear chair legs.
My dad dangled his ugly, bare feet. They were big and*

the soles were so thick that his toes didn't touch the floor, and the skin was dry and scaly. He went barefoot except when he had a job, and then he wore thick-soled, high-top work shoes. Sitting on the porch steps, I stared at my dad's feet. I hated his feet. I hated when I had to handle his smelly work boots and socks.

There were times when I hated him with all the fury a ten year old could feel. Like the time he was supposed to take me to swim at a new pool in the city park. He'd worked a job as a W.P.A. crew member building the pool, and now that it was open, he said he'd take me back with him after lunch so I could swim. I sat on the front porch for almost three hours, with my bathing suit wrapped in a worn towel, waiting for him. But he'd gone drinking instead. His two-day bender also cost him his job. I didn't have any affection for him at all; I tolerated him.

The third violent outburst between Dad and the landlord was prompted when the landlord said, "You know, Charlie, if you wouldn't spend so much money on wine you could pay the rent."

Dad got mad. Here was the landlord drinking the wine Charlie had paid for and then telling him he shouldn't spend so much money on wine. His face began to get purple; his lips tightened in a straight line; he brought the chair legs down with a crash and slapped the landlord right across the mouth with the back of his hand and then staggered upstairs toward our apartment.

The landlord followed him, shouting obscenities. At the top of the stairs, the two men struggled drunkenly. Dad lost his balance and tumbled down the stairs, his head bumping along the steps and his bulbous nose bleeding profusely. The landlord stumbled and fell down the stairs behind him, and landed on top of Dad. They crashed wildly at the bottom of the stairs where I was standing, too terrified to move.

The sound of the police siren on that Sunday was a welcome sound. It signaled the end of the drinking and fighting for at least a little while. Everybody laughs at the drunk, but it's not funny.

That night, my mother, my dad's sister, and I went to the courthouse. Mother had to bring Dad's shoes, before he could go before the judge. We sat in the back row of the crowded courthouse and listened to other cases brought before the judge. Eventually, the side door opened and a policeman brought Dad and the landlord into the courtroom. They were still wearing their blood-spattered clothes, but each had combed his hair and Charlie had his shoes on. I looked at my mother and knew she saw the fear in my eyes. My legs were shaking inside and my stomach felt like I was on a Ferris wheel ride. I wasn't scared because Dad had been arrested or that he might be put in jail; I was scared because of what my mother wanted me to do.

My aunt had told my mother to make me speak to the judge explaining that if Dad went to jail he would lose his job and we couldn't pay the rent. My aunt must have thought the judge would be impressed with a little girl pleading to keep her daddy out of jail. Both she and my mother didn't know that I didn't care if he went to jail.

The judge was quietly talking to Charlie and the landlord and listening to what they had to say. It wasn't a new story to the judge; he heard it every day. The judge was silent for a few moments as he reread the officer's report. Then he raised his eyes and looked straight at both of them and said, "Maybe ten days in jail will help you dry-out and cool your tempers."

Mother prodded me, "Go on, June. Tell the judge what I told you."

I looked at my mother and thought about ten days without Dad, without sending me to the liquor store, without him drinking. I also thought about his smelly feet and said, "I'm not gonna do it."

Reflecting on this story, I can't help but think of my mom's love of peanuts. Oh my gosh! My mom loved peanuts! It's no wonder her father could bribe her. For her, the best part of flying on an airplane was receiving the package of peanuts. The thrill was never the same when all she got was pretzels. At home, she'd purchase a jar or can of peanuts and try to ration her consumption. She'd commit to taking just a reasonable portion, a small snack. But then she'd take another, and then another, and soon the jar would be empty. She was a peanut-aholic!

The story also reflects a day-in-the-life of living with an

alcoholic father, at least a day of not being the targeted recipient of the trauma it presented. She was a ten-year-old kid, playing jacks on the front porch beside two men getting sloshed. Almost as a spectator, she viewed the scene; the police coming multiple times, the men hiding their bottles, the drunken brawl. She had no choice but to tolerate his very existence. When she did have a choice, in court, she took it.

Throughout my mom's undergraduate education, I didn't read her writing assignments. A few times I'd looked over her shoulder while she was typing, and she'd covered up her paper with a slight, embarrassed giggle. I never specifically asked to read her work, and therefore, she never specifically said I couldn't, but she didn't leave her work exposed on the table either. She didn't want us to know of all her childhood traumas until she thought we were mature enough or until she felt she could relay them with a perspective she sought to gain through writing. Even though I've scanned these stories before, I read them now with a gentler, more engaged ear, and some of her writings bring to light new information, even new perspectives.

THE NEBRASKA FLU

The first time I recall alcohol entering the sphere of my life was when I was eight years old. It was our first year in New Zealand. While I wouldn't have been privy to adult pressures with regard to alcohol in the military culture, studies support its existence.

My parents did not drink alcohol, and it was generally not in our home. I know from stories told later that my mother was a sobering influence (pun intended) on my stepfather. She encouraged her faith and her clean living patterns, and at times he was overcome with emotional gratitude. He would cry real tears and speak of my mother being the best thing that ever happened to him. But he weakened in New Zealand.

If he didn't come home right after work, my mom's stress level would build as the evening hours inched by. Her mouth grew tense; her jaw clenched. This particular evening rings clear in my memory. My mother was telephoned and had to drive out to the military base to pick up my stepfather, as he was too drunk to drive. I recall having to use the bathroom and the window was open, so I heard their voices in the backyard when they returned. He was retching on the lawn and couldn't stand up. He was really drunk and, while I didn't know what "drunk" was, it was scary.

He was begging her for help and said, "Barb, don't let the kids see me like this."

My mom was steady in her resolve of disgust. He made it into the house and stood at the entrance to the living room where we kids were watching TV; I think he even waved an unsteady hello and then went upstairs. That he was standing was in stark contrast to what I'd heard from the window just moments earlier. I'll bet we all looked like ghosts, frozen in place, staring at him. No one got up, no one said "Hi Daddy"; we all just stayed glued in position.

The next morning, the smell of vomit permeated our one bathroom, as he had vomited all over the wallpapered wall behind the toilet. That smell and the stain on the wallpaper were reminders of that night for the rest of the year we lived in that house.

My parents rarely went out socially. Most entertainment funds were reserved for family activities—road trips or a rare family movie attendance. Movies only cost a shilling, which equated to about a quarter. Quite often, they played cards with other military couples in the evenings. Alcohol was consumed, much to my mother's annoyance, but we kids were always in bed before the end of their bridge playing.

Our third and last year in New Zealand brought a second memory of a spike in this struggle. My mom had a good friend who was slightly younger. Her husband worked with my stepfather. My folks played cards with them, we road-tripped with them, and they had kids the same ages as my younger siblings. While alcohol was not the nucleus of the couples' friendship, it was present on occasion. One day, I came home and my mom was on the phone with this friend. Guilty of seeking affection, I liked to kneel on the floor beside my mother and lay my head on her lap while she sat in a chair and talked on the phone. She would absentmindedly run her fingers through my hair, repeatedly combing the hair around the top of my ear. It felt good, and since she so rarely showed physical affection, I took advantage of this opportunity more than once.

I wasn't listening to her conversation, although I could certainly hear it. My attention piqued, though, when I heard her say, "I've made a mistake before, and I think I've made another one."

She was referring to her first and now second marriages. There's a quandary within the memory. This one comment stuck with me as it alluded to a possible major change on the horizon, yet I felt no fear, no worry of loss. I was eleven years old and knew my mom would always be with me. I had never developed that assurance in a dad.

When we got back to the US, we purchased a car in California and drove across the country to Virginia, our next military tour of duty. The road trip included numerous stops to visit and spend the night with friends and some relatives of my stepfather's in Nebraska. That's when she hatched the "Nebraska flu" idea. The Nebraska flu was offered to my younger siblings as the illness explanation for his hangovers. We weren't in the bar, viewing the consumption; we only saw the day-after malady.

My mom said, "If anyone drank that much water, they'd be ill."

Once settled in Virginia, this issue seemed to calm for a while. We ate dinner every evening as a family and watched television every evening as a family. Once or twice a week, they continued to play cards in the evenings with other couples, but again, if consumption of alcohol was excessive, it was after we were in bed. The navy officer my stepfather was replacing in Virginia was a family man, with kids of similar ages to us, and they attended a local Methodist church. Again, while not privy to adult conversations surrounding the decision, we began attending the same church, and my stepfather was actually baptized in that church. Perhaps this act was his ante-in to their consolation. His commute to work was well over an hour, so the officer's club happy hour was less convenient. He did drink on occasion, but I have no memory of a blowup.

After two years, we moved to Orange County, California, and he was stationed aboard ship, away from home. For a variety of reasons, different for every member of the family, this was a difficult time. For me, the major difficulty was adjusting to the Southern California hippie culture in 1969–70, after two years in conservative Virginia and three years prior in the time warp of New Zealand.

But in the home with just Mom and us kids, everything seemed calm, and she went about our daily routines with steady normalcy.

We had one more military post assignment, back to the east coast, this time on the Maryland side of Washington, DC. Here I attended and graduated high school. I am the only kid in my family who attended one high school for all four years. After twenty years in the navy, my stepfather retired and went to college full-time. To be accurate, he went double-time. He completed the balance of his bachelor's degree (having earned maybe one year's credits from night courses) and his master's degree in accounting in just three years.

I spoke of his accomplishment with great pride. He was smart and self-disciplined in this pursuit. His course load of forty-five or more credit hours in any given semester required special dispensation from the university. Our family of six functioned on only his military retirement income for those three years. My mom and older sister also received paid tuition. We were never without milk in the refrigerator, or toilet paper, toothpaste, and tissue in every bathroom.

While we were not permitted to use a car for pleasure or spend any money on what they assessed as frivolous, the words "we can't afford it" were not spoken. The phrases "it's not necessary" or "you don't need it" were the mantras. My parents' self-control was extraordinary. Mom gets most of the credit for managing expenses, as she did ninety percent of the buying.

They never owned a credit card and always paid cash for any vehicle. We had clean, albeit mostly home-sewn, clothes. Mom sewed beautiful lined draperies for every room in our house every time we moved. Our furniture was simple and inexpensive, but not junk. They tracked and logged every nickel and rarely made any personal spending choice that might impede the needs of the family. Their choice of needs included music lessons, braces, participation in sports, three cars, and air conditioning. Although we weren't doing without, we kids still bemoaned the lack of money granted for our adolescent whims.

Chronically moving is particularly difficult during adolescence. Fashion changed drastically from British school-uniformed New Zealand to penny loafers and Peter Pan collars in Virginia, to Peter Max psychedelic Orange County in the 1970s, then back to preppy DC suburbia, all within five years. Those needs were not indulged and we viewed these forbiddances as mean. It's all relative. Today, kids feel deprived without the newest technology device; we felt deprived for not being allowed a dime for a candy bar. I'm still in awe of their accomplishment as a couple in their discipline and steadfast intent of educational goals.

Once we moved to Minnesota, my stepfather's weakness to drink resurfaced. Sometimes I thought he was just a wimpy drinker, that he couldn't hold his booze, as was the often articulated criticism in the world of alcohol. Sometimes I thought my mom was extreme in her judgment. In letters from her years later, she wrote of having hidden his drinking from us kids, so my criticism of her intolerance may have been an illusion. Even as a kid, I knew by my mother's face if she was annoyed. Nothing could hide her annoyance for alcohol. She could never have hidden her reactions from us. If we didn't observe the drinking, we surely saw the hangover. Complete with him pleading for a grilled cheese sandwich and soup. Mom gritted her teeth, and with her jaw set, she provided the food, if only to shut him up.

Mom would never acknowledge degrees with regard to alcohol. She saw abstinence or drunkard, with nothing in between. It is of no surprise that once Mom could remove the existence of alcohol from her life, she did.

WOULD YOU COCKTAIL?

I watched the waitress working the lounge at the Ramada Inn and I was intrigued. She looked like an adult, but she wasn't any older than I was. I perceived her to be more grown-up because of her job serving alcohol to patrons sitting at small, round tables in a darkened room. The opposite ends of the lounge were slightly brighter, with a U-shaped bar at one end and a small stage for live musicians at the other. We'd arrived in Minnesota just a few days prior, and while our family was having dinner in the Ramada dining room with my folks' friends, I was deciding my next employment opportunity.

We'd moved from Maryland with the legal drinking age at twenty-one to Minnesota with legal drinking at eighteen. I was nineteen, so I was one year behind the curve of consumption and I'd never sat in a bar. I would be attending the local state college, entering my sophomore year, but I needed a job for spending money and wanted a job for independence. I was hired as a coffee shop waitress with the opportunity to work banquets on occasion. This was one step down from a dining room waitress and presumptively further down from the lounge staff. They displayed swagger, even when sober.

My mom was fine with my choice of job, excited for me as always. Neither of us knew how easily it would roll into job advancement and then career choice. I quickly got the hang of waitressing, and I was good at it. No complaints from my customers, and I even had "call customers," hotel guests who requested a specific waitress. I worked hard, always available to pick up extra shifts when the boss called.

One evening after about three weeks of employment, the food and beverage director approached me just as my coffee shop shift was ending and asked, "Would you like to cocktail?"

First of all, I didn't know the word cocktail was a verb. Secondly, I knew nothing about alcohol. Nada! Jack-squat. And lastly, he meant right now, this minute, in the lounge.

I had probably had three tastes of alcohol in my life, all in the last year and all sparked by the presence of others versus my own volition. Once I tasted a rum and Coke with my boyfriend's friends, once a Singapore Sling when out to dinner with a friend's alcoholic mother who encouraged that we have a drink, and once a Tom Collins, when a friend and I boldly walked into the enlisted men's club on the small navy base where I worked in the mess hall. I was equally complicit in the last outing; while my friend may have initiated the idea, I had access to the base. All occasions were sips, never finishing the one drink. My mom had put the fear of God in me regarding alcohol. I don't know what I was more afraid of—getting caught by my mom or what alcohol might do to me.

Since alcohol was rarely present in our house and only on hand for those infrequent social occasions when guests would consume, *and* since my mother saw no purpose to it at all, I wasn't provided any knowledge. Entrance into the land of adult-beverage felt like an entrance into adulthood, and I was seeking adulthood. So, I agreed to cocktail that night.

I just love restaurant people. Through the past fifty years, ninety percent of all memories with co-workers, peers, supervisors, and reports are filled with the generosity of heart common among most of us. That "aptitude to serve" is such a kind personality trait and what drew me into the profession. Those first few evenings cocktailing intensely engaged my consciousness and my dreams. Everyone in the business knows of "waiter dreams"—when you wake with a start, dreaming of trying to organize the countless tasks running through your head to get the job done. One time, early on in this work, I bolted upright in bed and began calling a drink order to a figment bartender.

The first few shifts, the bartender, Allison, was trying to teach me the specifics of booze while I was running back and forth from ten occupied tables to their bar-rail, balancing my sixteen-inch round tray filled with replacement drinks or empties. I was supposed to verbally order the drinks I needed for patrons in a specific order of spirit category and production complexity, but I didn't even know there were categories within all of those bottles! I didn't know that Johnnie Walker Black was a Scotch whiskey. So I didn't grasp the tiers of well brands to call brands to premium brands. I knew nothing! When I approached the bar-rail servers' station, I would do my best to repeat precisely what the customer at a table had requested. That first night, I was the unsuspecting comedic entertainment for all the guests sitting at Allison's bar. They all burst out laughing when I said, "I need a chinkas wrinkle on the rocks." It was a Chivas Regal. Good old Allison, so patient with my ignorance.

Within a few weeks, I was full-time in the lounge, no longer a less prestigious coffee shop waitress. Within a few months, I was bartending. I was fast, accurate, and I had a good memory. Two cocktailers and multiple dining room servers could verbally order countless drinks, walk away to tend to other tasks, and come back to all drinks ready and correct. I just had it: an aptitude for the business.

Of course, bar business work comes with a lifestyle. We consumed alcohol, and we consumed other "under the influence" substances. Back then, most all of us smoked cigarettes. We were vampires, awake until four or five o'clock in the morning and sleeping until noon the next day. We were tough. I've never met a bartender yet, who didn't have that swagger.

My mother would have been appalled, devastated, and angry had she known about some of these habits. They surely would have cut off financial support to my education, and she probably would have had me committed, given her intolerance. Like I said, I escaped lasting consequences by the skin of my teeth from some stupid decisions and actions. But early on, all of this was energizing, exciting, rewarding, and completely new to me. I loved it and changed my major to hospitality management by the time I completed my sophomore year.

There was no teaching, no guidance, no discussion about alcohol in our home except that of total abstinence. My mom saw no grey. Prohibition was her stance. I overconsumed a number of times in early adulthood. I drove while impaired more times than I'd like to admit, and with relaxed inhibitions, I made some poor choices. I cannot blame any of my dumb, reckless choices on her lack of guidance. Her mantra was abstinence; I just didn't follow it.

In the last decade or so, I credit the fear she instilled as the threshold I will not cross. Even with those bad choices, I can count my hangovers on one hand. Four were in my twenties. If I have the gene identified as alcoholism, it is recessive. I've discovered a shutoff valve in my throat after a drink or two, maximum half of a third. I just don't want more. I can't think of one time when overconsumption brought out the best in a person or a situation. Not one.

I rarely consume alcohol today, and I don't waste any time in the presence of a drunk. I was promoted to dining room manager after eighteen months bartending. I have a suspicion the promotion, while deserving, may have been an answer to remove me from the bar. I had heard the accusation of my being "cutoff happy," not allowing customers to overconsume.

I choose to have my wits about me, making my decisions and actions with a clear head. Some people may say it's a control issue, and I have to agree. I like to be in control of me. In control to extricate myself when necessary versus control anyone else.

My mom was placed, without choice, on the hard road to her long-suffering position. I took the long road, going off in the ditch a few times, but finished much closer to her end-game than I ever thought I would.

IV

On Men

IT'S A LACK OF TRUST!

Discussions on boy-girl relationships or sexuality didn't happen. We just didn't have those conversations. I don't know of anyone from the 1960s who received information from their mother, and mine was no different. Mom didn't allow herself, or perhaps flatter herself, or even expose herself as being sexually attractive. Once, when my sister and I were sixteen and thirteen years old, we were going shopping by ourselves, as Mom didn't shop other than for groceries. My stepfather was due to come home from a six-month tour of duty aboard an aircraft carrier. She struggled when she asked us to purchase something for her.

"I need a pair of slippers ... you know ... something pretty, a little ..." And my sister interjected, "Sexy?" We all had a little nervous giggle at the thought of Mom and sexy. We found her a pair of turquoise, slip-on, kitten-heeled satin slippers with poufy pompons on top of the toes. My mind didn't wander any further with regard to her intention, other than looking pretty and feminine.

Her life lessons regarding the birds and the bees had been even less than mine. Each subsequent generation has broadened in this teaching. However, the lessons regarding "stranger danger" have also increased with equal or greater emphasis. Topics of evil sexual intent, which were once taboo, are now commonplace. That's a good thing. Mom's story of traversing the streets of south Los Angeles, alone as a kid, reflects that evil is evil, any year, any day.

Saturday Matinee

*I was ten years old and used to being on my own.
I walked easily down Main Street in Los Angeles
completely naïve, confidant, and unafraid. I knew where
I was going and what I was doing. I was on my way
to the movies on a Saturday afternoon with enough
money to pay for my movie ticket and some left over for
a package of my favorite chewy Walnettos.*

*Hadn't decided which movie to go see – guess
it would depend on what the stage show was. The
Hippodrome Theatre usually had a good stage show,
and it was the closest theatre so I'd probably go there. I
bought my ticket and groped my way into the darkened
theatre to find a seat.*

*I was engrossed in the movie when I became aware
of a jingling noise. Sitting next to me was a small boy of
five or six and seated next to him was his father, a small
thin dark haired man. The man had his hand in his
pants pocket and was jingling his pocket change.*

*The father handed some money to his boy and whis-
pered something in his ear and the boy left. Pretty soon
the boy came back with his hands full of candy. I was
glad he had returned because I had begun to feel uncomfortable because his father kept glancing over my way
and jingling money in his pockets. After a few moments
the father reached his arm across the little boy and with
a sly grin offered me a pack of Necco Wafers.*

I shook my head and refused the candy – couldn't figure out why he wanted to give me candy.

Before long the father whispered in his son's ear again and the little boy got up and traded seats with his father. Now that creep was sitting next to me and jingling that money in his pockets. The Hippodrome was three-quarters empty, so why did that guy have to sit next to me – he could have any seat in the house. I decided to leave. I got up as nonchalantly as was possible for a ten year old and walked out of the theatre into the welcome daylight and safety.

I knew I should go home, but it was still early in the afternoon and Dad was probably drunk by now and that was the reason Mom sent me to the movies; to get away from Dad, and besides I still had fifteen cents.

I ambled south on Main Street trying to decide if I should go to another movie. After walking a few blocks I saw a marquis advertising a Mickey Rooney movie I hadn't seen, and I liked to see all of his movies. I paid my ten cents for the ticket and entered a darkened theatre again. This movie house was much smaller than the Hippodrome and in shabby condition. I found a seat on the front row, which pleased me (but always distressed my mother), and sat down to watch my matinee idol.

It wasn't long until a man sat down beside me. He was big and fat with a big nose and a pock-marked face that looked sinister, especially in the dim light of the movie screen. After a while the big man got up and made his way up the center aisle to the back of the theatre. A feeling of relief came over me and this surprised me. Guess I still felt jumpy about that incident at the Hippodrome.

I scarcely had time to get my attention back to the movie when the big man plopped down next to me again, brushing his legs against mine. I felt a twinge of fear. Suddenly the big man thrust a bar of candy at me.

I shook my head, but he insisted, "Look, little girl, I just thought you'd like some candy. I'm not going to hurt you."

I hesitated and then reluctantly took the candy. I was a little hungry since I had spent all my money on movie tickets and hadn't bought any candy. Darn that man at the Hippodrome! Now I didn't have money for candy and I wouldn't get to see the stage show either. Darn him!

I munched at the candy and began to feel a bit secure, and at least this man wasn't jingling money in his pocket. He raised his arms to stretch and when he brought them down again one of them was across the back of my seat.

"You know you're a cute girl. Did anyone ever give you a screen test for the movies?"

I shook my head, too scared to open my mouth.

"You know, I'm a talent scout, and that's my job, just looking around for cute girls so I can take them to the movie studio and put them in the movies. I'll bet you'd like to be in the movies."

I nodded. Anybody who spent as much time at the movies as I did was certain to be stage struck. Maybe he really was a talent scout. He talked quietly for a little while trying to impress me with all the movie stars he knew and then I heard it.

"I'll tell you what. You come with me and I'll get my car and we'll go out to MGM and give you a screen test."

That word "car" was the clue. What had Mother always told me? "Don't take candy from strangers," which I had done, "and don't ever get in a car with a strange man." Now I knew for certain. This man wasn't a talent scout. He was lying to me. How was I going to get away?

The big man kept talking and his arm slyly touched my shoulder. I jumped up, muttering something about going to the bathroom and ran up the darkened aisle. Mid-way up the aisle of the narrow theatre was a cross aisle that led to restrooms on either side. I quickly turned left and dashed into the ladies' room. I was panting for breath and too scared to move. I waited in the restroom for about ten minutes, even though it seemed an eternity before I gathered enough courage to go out the door.

Slowly I opened the door and carefully walked out. My heart stopped as I glanced over my right shoulder and could see by the light from the screen that the seat

where that horrid man had been sitting was now empty.
Where was he? Was he waiting in the dark lobby to grab
me? I had no choice. I ran the rest of the way up the
dark aisle and out into the sweet and friendly sunlight
and sprinted for home without a backward glance. I was
too scared to look.

When I arrived at our apartment I was out of breath
and my face was white as chalk. Mother looked up,
surprised, and said, "What's the matter, June?"

What could I say?

Such irony in this story: Fannie sent June to the movies to keep
her safe from the inevitability of her drunken father, only for her to
be met with a similar ilk. Furthermore, Barbara, as an adult writing
this story from memory, totally negated this juxtaposition. She
was accustomed to threatening "normal" behavior from her father,
but her mother was there to protect her. On her own, a stranger's
behavior presented a raised awareness of her mother's warnings
and gave her the ability to self-protect.

She gained defensive skills into adolescence. She told about a
time when she and her best friend, Idean, were walking home from
school after dark, having attended an evening activity. They were
being followed by a man in military uniform, and he was drunk.
They crossed to the other side of the street and then he crossed.
They crossed back, and he crossed back. Idean was timid and scared
beyond the ability to reason. June had learned "how to handle the
drunk" from her mother. June turned around, pointed her finger at
this soldier, and said, "What do you think you're doing, following

us?! You just get out of here and leave us alone!" She'd learned well. As a ten-year-old, she knew flight, but as a thirteen-year-old, she chose fight.

In a letter to me dated September 2, 1986, almost fifty years later, she wrote:

Since I was in this strange (but predictable and familiar) mood, it was certainly not the time to see a Phil Donahue show on incest and sexual abuse. We rarely seem to mention it anymore - - I don't know if that's good or bad - - but every time I see a program about these topics, I get angry all over again. My heart hurts for you and it's such a helpless feeling. And then I grieve for myself too, since none of us have escaped.

In the process of thinking through so many crazy events in my life, I began to wonder about my father. I never felt comfortable with him and I never knew why – and still don't - - but I wonder if he didn't abuse me when I was a toddler. Something must have happened to make me feel strange around him. I had a flash of a memory of when I was about seven and I woke up one night and sensed that someone was in the room. I was afraid to move, but I remember seeing the outline of my father just standing in my room and I could see the red end of a burning cigarette. I never knew why he was there.

I guess the saddest part of it all is that from these miserable experiences you lose trust. I never really thought about that, but the psychiatrist on the

Donahue show kept stressing that point. I think I've always labeled it as being a man-hater, but in reality it is a lack of trust in men. Probably starting with my father, and then all those creeps that I ran away from while I lived in Los Angeles; another group of creeps that entered my life while I was in high school.

My mother did washing for a family and the man started coming by on Saturday morning to pick up the laundry for the family (wife and three kids) and then he would come into the one bedroom that we had and I always slept late on Saturday morning. I knew what he had in mind. But I was a kid, what gave him the right to just walk in the house like that!? How can a kid behave rationally against that type of thing? It seemed like there was always somebody around who wanted to give me rides to school – many times they were men in our church. Pretty soon any dumb fool can see a pattern when a man always seems to be driving down a certain street at exactly the same time you're going to school. Don't get me wrong – I never had any delusions about my appearance because this type of adult behavior is not a compliment. I guess there is one consolation that I feel right now; your molester is burning in hell.

When we were living in Virginia, outside of Washington, DC, I suffered a molestation experience. Living in such a historic part of the country is a bit like living in a resort on the beach; friends and family want to visit and take in the sights. In this case, sights of our nation's capital. My mother bent over backward to provide excellence in her tour-guide services for the multiple families who visited our home. She knew how to contact the various state representatives or senate offices to secure seats in the gallery of the Senate or House of Representatives. She knew how to secure tickets for a White House tour, or where to park, or which Smithsonian Institute Museum was of greatest interest to a specific family of houseguests. All sourcing of information was accomplished through phone calls and letter writing, as there was no internet in the late 1960s. Let me just say, I rode in the way-back of a station wagon, packed with up to ten people in the middle of summer, many, many times! I saw the FBI Building tour seven times in our two-year tour of duty in Virginia.

One of our visiting families was my stepfather's older sister, her husband, and their two sons, from a rural, small farming town in Nebraska. I was always excited about "company coming." My brother and I would sit on the curb at the corner of our street, watching for the headlights of the car that would eventually be the right one. We'd run back up the sidewalk to greet them as they pulled into the driveway. So my excitement was surely out there in the open. It's just who I was ... or am.

I'd willingly given my bedroom to a cousin, and my sister had given hers to the aunt and uncle (bears noting, they didn't sleep together in their own home, but my mother drew the line in trying to make accommodation to whatever their issue was). I was to sleep on the same basement level, in the rec room on a sofa, which was really a twin bed with bolster pillows.

The first morning after their arrival, I awoke to my uncle

touching me. I could hear my mother and others talking upstairs in the kitchen, preparing breakfast. His brazenness still blows my mind. He touched, he kissed, he talked ... let's just say he tried third base, but I started to freak out. He was obese, old, and ugly. He had a barrel-shaped body, wore dungaree overalls all the time, and he had dentures that clicked chronically. It was disgusting.

After breakfast was over, I silently, gingerly, in a fog, walked down the hall and into my mother's room. She was taking a shower in her bathroom.

I said, "Mom ..." And I have no memory of the words I chose to relay the nastiness. I only recall her pulling back the shower curtain so I could see her face and she could see mine, and she said, "He *what*?!"

That night, and the few after that for the length of their visit, I slept on the same upper level as my mother. I slept in my younger sister's room. I was emotional and off and on shook with fear. My mother was in and out of my room numerous times throughout that first night while I wept and cried. Exposing the step-uncle's crime, denouncing his actions, and risking family strife simply did not happen. Therefore, I was expected to sit at a dinner table and ride in a car with my molester for the remaining days of their visit. Had she not been married to my stepfather, I believe she would have shown her passion in action, as I believe I would, had I been in her shoes.

She told me that she confronted my uncle. "Touch my daughter again, and I'll kill you." I didn't hear her say this, but I believed her. She might have even told me she was holding a knife when she said it, or maybe that was only in my imagination as I embraced the protection of her words.

We've all heard it said, "When a child is sexually abused, it changes who they are." Even Dr. Phil repeats this claim. Sometime shortly after my own violation, when I was twelve or thirteen, our family went to see the Barnum & Bailey Circus.

I was sitting with my sister one row ahead of the rest of the family. I saw the old man clown ambling up the aisle stairs and felt my tension rising to the point that I felt dizzy. I looked away from him but kept an awareness of him. All the people in our section were watching him and laughing. As he got closer and closer to me, I grew more and more nervous. My face must have shown this; it must have shown fear.

He sat on my lap, trying to get me to look at him and faking that he was going to kiss me. I was frozen, trying to ignore him, trying to escape mentally and emotionally from the situation while he had me trapped physically.

To this day, I don't know how I got through it. The seating area was packed with people. Why did he choose me? It's beyond my comprehension that any man can look in the face of a child who is expressing such paralyzing fear and have it mean nothing or have no compassion. I'll never understand.

I've often wondered what my mother thought at the time; we never talked about it. There was nothing she could have said or done, but she surely must have seen my discomfort. She always said, "I can read your face a mile away." Maybe she thought if she didn't acknowledge or validate my fear, it would fade away. It didn't. I was leery of older men for many years. In my forties, my advanced age also advanced my perception of what was "older." Realizing I could physically overtake an old man if need be lessened my fear.

Somehow my mom navigated her way through her distrust of men and was married, not once but twice. That's not to say twice is a success story, but more to say she trusted a man to the point of marriage on two occasions. Oh, I don't think every man has evil intent, but I know my vigilance is there in the back of my mind, especially when a little girl is present. I've yet to find my way through that distrust. You know, if it walks like a duck and quacks like a duck, it's a darn duck! I've met more than my fair share of mallards.

DID YOU LOVE HIM?

Every kid has a desire to know how their parents met, to discover their romance story. Knowledge of my biological parents' courtship was a completely avoided topic. The only time his name was spoken was in reference to scheduling visitation with my sister and me. When en route to our next military post, we'd stop in San Diego, and my mother arranged a visit. He was referred to as Ralph, his first name, within the walls of our home. On the rare occasion when I was able to learn something about how my parents came to be married, the story didn't add up to romance.

After high school, June attended a local junior college. She had been dating a young man named David, and they even had been officially engaged. But something, somehow, or someone reneged on the engagement. At the end of World War II, in 1945, all the boys were coming back from the war. Most all of June's friends were getting married.

June had been an active high school student. She was in numerous clubs and activities and had a large circle of close friends. In

fact, six or seven of those girls created their own club called the
P.L.I.B.s and swore each other to secrecy regarding the meaning
of the acronym. Their club was sanctioned by the school, and they
had letterman sweaters with the club name monogrammed, yet no
one knew what it meant. Those cheeky girls: the **P**rotection **L**eague
for **I**nnocent **B**oys. She kept in touch with all of those women
for her whole life. And, of course, she had that voice, her singing
ability, her "claim to fame," her confidence builder. But what was
that doing for her now?

June met Ralph through her friend Idean. Idean was getting
married and Ralph was a friend of a cousin of the groom. While
my suspicions are all speculative, I think June was feeling stagnant.
Everyone was getting married, her mother had remarried two years
earlier, high school was over, and her circle of friends and activities
were forever changed. I think she fell in line, versus fell in love.

Ralph's family was not wealthy, but with steady work and a
devout family structure, his upbringing had been without the
hardships June had endured. He had an older brother and a sister
one year younger. Ralph and June married, and evidenced by the
newspaper clipping Ralph kept all of his life, I can deduce his family
absorbed most of the expense.

He was a blue-collar tradesman, factory work I believe, and
eventually became a foreman in a tool and dye factory. However,
on the rare occasion of telling, Mom's stories reeked of him being
controlling. They bought property in Ontario, California, and
built a house, and I mean *they* built it.

Ontario is part of the sprawl of Southern California today, but
it was the boonies back then. Ralph went to work and June stayed

home, with no telephone, no car, no radio, nothing—by herself, alone all day in the boonies. Every Sunday, they'd go to his family's home. Mom felt belittled by his parents, as they were always flaunting Ralph's sister as being better than Mom at everything. Her impoverished upbringing was on her like a stench, or so they made her feel.

Ralph and June were married five years before having their first child. Once, in a senior moment of long-term memory revealed, Mom told me they were married six months before they "did it." I think my eyes popped out of my head in disbelief because she shut up after that comment. Had I been less startled, she may have revealed more details. I could speculate he was a mama's boy, a grown man who still saw himself through the eyes of his mother as a six-year-old boy.

I asked her, "Did you love him at the time of the marriage?" She replied, "I thought I did."

Sometime in my young adult years, I asked my mom why she divorced him. What happened? Did he hit her, did he abuse her, what can cause a twenty-eight-year-old woman, with two kids under the age of three, in 1955, with no job and no car, to think, "I'm out of here"? Her reply was, "I just wasn't going to live like that."

Although she'd had her fill of spending every Sunday with his family, and she'd put up with her "solitary confinement" for eight years, I think the straw that broke the camel's back was when she wanted to gift her mother a cloth coat for Christmas, and he said no. The snub, the control, still burned in her mind when she told me, "A lousy cloth coat!"

I related to this with regard to the use of the telephone. In the late 1970s, when I was just a couple of years into adulthood, I called my mom a lot, and we'd talk for a long time. Long distance wasn't free; it was downright expensive. When I first moved out, I couldn't even afford the forty-dollar deposit required for a telephone line until after my third paycheck. I would drive to the Denny's restaurant not far from my apartment and shove quarters, *lots* of quarters, into the pay phone to talk weekly with my mom on my day off. Once I had a phone, while still not making much money, I'd incur phone bills in excess of one hundred dollars without blinking an eye. My gross pay was seven hundred and seventy-five dollars a month, and my rent was two hundred and fifty dollars a month. Do the math.

Mom would chide me, saying, "This is costing you a fortune."

I never listened to her caution or criticism of my phone bills. In fact, I said, "No man will ever tell me I can't talk to my mother any time I want and for as long as I want." I think she even believed me when I said, "I'd rather talk with you than buy two new pairs of shoes."

The absurdity was that no man was telling me anything, but I was already building the defenses. The pattern is not lost on me here. Knowledge of her resistance to Ralph's control and taking a stance on my choice in "phone spending" did not occur simultaneously or even within years of each other. However, the lesson to never allow a man control over my life was taught and learned just the same. Here I was, taking a defiant position without even the glint of a cause. It was *her* cause, not mine, but I embraced it and modeled it.

After June left Ralph, we lived in National City, California. She met and befriended a young couple with two girls very close in age to my sister and me. They were all friends until the end. She got a job as a secretary, actually stretching the truth about her shorthand skills in the interview.

In a letter dated February 7, 1985, she recalled this time in her life:

> When I went to work when you were a baby, I was only concerned about making a house payment and buying food. I knew there would never be enough money for many clothes, and I didn't even have a car. It was really a struggle – I had to take the bus to work in San Diego and didn't get home from work until after six p.m. Your sister was three and a half and she would be waiting by the front window with her Mickey Mouse ears on – she knew that once the Mickey Mouse club T.V. show was over, I would be coming home. I hated it that you began to call the babysitter "Mama."
>
> Then after we moved to that little cracker-box in Chula Vista, things really got tight. During the job change, I went three weeks without a paycheck, and the last paycheck from my previous job was short because I had spent that week looking for a job. During that year, you kids had measles, chicken pox, tonsillitis, flu, and hives.
>
> In spite of all that, I always felt that I was in control to a certain extent. When you don't have much, you don't have much to control. Edna Mae and Lehnis were such good friends during that time. There was never

an offer of money—that was not even something either
of us considered. They used to come and get me and
both you girls and we'd go back to their house and
have dinner and talk, and talk, and talk. When I finally
managed to get a car (I think it cost one hundred and
fifty dollars), Lehnis felt bad because it looked so bad
and he didn't want Ralph to think that I had to buy a
piece of junk, so we put it in their garage and all three of
us waxed it up just great. I paid twenty dollars a month
until it was paid-off.

You didn't know you were going to get this nostalgia
trip—I didn't know it either. However, it always bothers
me that you are alone with nobody to share the prob-
lems. I guess I was alone too, but I don't remember feel-
ing so alone. It was a relief to be on my own (much as
it is a relief today to only have to be concerned with my
own decisions and no compromises). Money is always
just a problem.

She was probably responding to something I might have written in a prior letter. Perhaps I bemoaned a feeling of aloneness in
dealing with the harsh realities of bills and responsibilities as a
single person. I know I felt that way sometimes, especially when
my peers were entering social couple-hood or even getting married.
At this time, she was celebrating her aloneness post her second
divorce. Never again having to worry about whether a husband
was happy with what they were doing, whom they were with, or
anything else.

Ralph had not wanted the divorce, and he was known to sit in his car on the street where we lived and watch for June. Today, that's stalking. This made her very uneasy. Once, a new girlfriend of Ralph's called my mom and was crying about how much he still loved her. Mom found this strange. The divorce wasn't amicable and conversely wasn't volatile. It just was. She never talked about it. She made her decision and that was that. Communication with him regarding visitation with my sister and me was sparse at best.

Ralph had visitation with my sister and me on Sundays. Of course, I don't have much memory of these weekly visits until I was closer to three years old. In later years, Mom revealed how she hated Sundays for all those years, fearing he would not bring us back. Another message learned of distrust toward men.

One of her jobs while newly divorced was on the naval base in San Diego. Sometimes she'd get a ride to and from work with her boss, who was also a young divorcee with one child. And sometimes her boss's boyfriend was driving the car. He became my stepfather.

Once again, kids want to know of the courtship of their parents. There's some illusion of them being completely different people, and we're intrigued. Since I was less than two years old when they married and had no knowledge of biological conception, in my mind, he was my dad.

Apparently, as my mom would get into the car, sliding into the center of the front bench seat, he noticed her legs and liked what he noticed. But since he was dating her boss, any attraction was ignored. Many months later, in October 1956, Mom was in the grocery store buying pumpkins for my sister and me, and he was there. He asked her out on a date. She was quite dumbfounded. I don't know whether she knew it at the time, but there was quite an age gap, to say nothing of the obvious gap in life experience. He was two months shy of his twenty-third birthday, and she was twenty-nine, divorced with two kids.

That night, she discussed his invitation with Edna Mae and Lehnis. Edna Mae said, "June, you should go. It's not like you're going to marry him, it's just a date."

They were married the following March. They spent a honeymoon weekend at Hotel Del Coronado, on Coronado Island—quite an extravagance to be sure.

Both came from nothing. Mom came from urban poverty, and he came from rural, Midwest, farm-country poverty. He was the last of nine children, often an annoyance to his older siblings who were saddled with the chores of farming. He joined the navy at just past seventeen years of age.

She brought her faith and the moral fiber of her life to their union. From his farm boy youth to navy enlisted man, complete with the stereotypical carousing of weekend liberty, he welcomed her guidance. And both sought education relentlessly, all of their lives. Both completed the coursework on their doctorates, and he completed the required finish work to earn a PhD. Fannie was forced to leave school after the third grade, and I doubt my step-father's mother had even completed that. This disparity in one generation is remarkable.

Before their first anniversary and shortly after my brother's birth, my step-father was deployed to Eniwetok. Just like in the movies when the military serviceman received R&R (rest and recreation), he was given little notice. A crackly telephone call to my mother, and they would be meeting in Hawaii within a day. My older sister and I were to stay with Edna Mae's mother and father, and my baby brother was staying with Edna Mae and Lehnis.

This is my first childhood memory. I'm sure we spent some social time with this grandparent couple, as I'm told we spent all our social time with Edna Mae, Lehnis, and their two daughters. However, my mom would have always been there. I've heard it said that our first memories are ones of high emotion or anxiety, so it makes sense to be memorable. This time she was leaving me. I recall being put in the deep back seat of an old, dark car. There was a small stuffed panda bear on the rear window ledge behind the back seat. I took hold of that toy and slunk down to a sitting position. I knew that bear was not mine, but I also knew no one was going to take it from me.

She wrote:

Yesterday my three children and I had started another lonely summer Sunday attending Sunday school and now tonight I find myself flying over the Pacific Ocean, heading for those long dreamed of Hawaiian Islands.

My husband had been on the small south Pacific island of Eniwetok for six months active duty with the Navy. Unexpectedly he was flown to Hawaii for a week of rest and recreation. Upon arriving in Hawaii, he placed a long distance call to me in Chula Vista, California, beseeching me to withdraw money from our savings account and fly to Hawaii to be with him.

My heart pounded in my ears with the anticipation of seeing my husband again and yet I felt a hesitation at leaving our three small children and flying off to what seemed at the time such a distant place. It had been a long and lonely six months for both of us, and now the possibility of being together again blotted out any sensible thoughts I might have had.

After hurried preparations were made and the children were happily settled with a sitter, I found myself on my way and beginning to have doubts as to the wisdom of this venture. I just wasn't sure that I should be on that plane traveling hundreds of miles away from my children, perhaps risking my life in that plane and spending too much money so frivolously and selfishly so that I could spend three short days with my husband.

Through the airplane window, even before we came to a complete stop, I caught a glimpse of my husband in his stark white Navy uniform. He appeared nervous, waiting for me. A bright yellow ginger flower lei was draped over his arm, to be placed around my neck. It seemed like hours before the doors finally opened and that sweet, floral, pineapple infused, balmy air reached my nose and my nervousness and excitement mounted. Once down the steps of the plane and hugging my husband close to me, I knew that for at least these few days, I was where I belonged. All my doubts and apprehensions were forgotten.

Both of them had an acute awareness of something better, a life of more security and privilege. His privilege included a home with indoor plumbing, something he hadn't known in farm life. Hers was to have a radio and a car. She demanded a car at her disposal even in the very early years. The idea of being trapped at home with small children was unacceptable. Even though she rarely went anywhere during the day, she needed to know she could.

They both liked music. I recall their first beyond-necessity purchase was a console stereo record player. They even bought the Ray Conniff Orchestra album that the salesman played to demonstrate the dual sound. They both liked to dance, and I enjoyed watching them. They danced so smoothly—no missteps. In 1965, about five years after the stereo purchase, they bought an Elvis Presley album and demonstrated something like the jitterbug in the middle of our living room while the four of us kids watched. Even in the mid-seventies, they took a disco-dancing class together. Mom was forty-eight and he was forty-one. I was twenty at the time and thought they were clearly too old to be taking disco lessons, but I also respected their self-assurance.

I believe they were in love. Undoubtedly, there were ups and downs in their marriage, times of peace and times of angst, but both believed in presenting a united front to us kids. We caught sight here and there of arguments or strife, but neither one ever spoke ill of the other openly to us. Mom made excuses to herself for his shortcomings and gave forgiveness.

Looking back, I've disagreed with some allowances she offered him. She wasn't as right as I always thought she was. She ran interference, but never, ever chose a position contrary to his with regard to parenting in front of us kids. She struggled with absolution for his worst offenses and worried her failure to forgive would prohibit her entrance to heaven. I prefer to think his sins were his to atone, as only God can grant such forgiveness and only to those who seek Him.

From a reliable source, I know June was crushed when her engagement to David ended. She was a senior in high school. She was a popular girl with lots of friends, athletic skills, and again, that singing voice. Her mother had married Henry, and she viewed him as an intrusion. Without positive paternal experience, I doubt she saw any value to his presence. Given all her hardships at the hands of men, it's plausible these ingrained biases contributed to strife within her marriages.

I've often looked back on this with a bit of wonder, a bit of awe. As much as I adored my mom and I think she was pretty and fun and smart, I wonder what specifically her two husbands saw in her. Perhaps I wonder because whatever they saw in her no man has ever seen in me. Whatever it was, it has eluded me. Although I have to say, I wouldn't have wanted either of them.

ACT DEMURE

Oh wait, I'm getting way ahead of myself. Similar to her guidance on alcohol, my mom imparted little instruction regarding the birds and the bees. At least with alcohol she had an abstinence stance, but regarding boy-girl relationships, she offered nothing.

When I came of age for my menstrual cycle, she called me into her bedroom and placed a new packaged sanitary belt and a pamphlet on the bed. That was it. There was no tolerance for PMS or even menstrual cramps. I suffered with cramps, and she accused me of having "talked to my friends" and said it was all in my head.

Once in a shoe store (again with the never-ending search for comfortable shoes), my brother irritated me, and I snapped at him. She murmured at me, "Are you having your period?" Then she followed with, "This is once a month for the rest of your life. Get a grip." Great lesson. Now that I've traversed the years of menopause, I'm quite certain she was in denial of that mood-altering passage also. She could be quite gnarly on occasion.

There was never any "Where did I come from?" communication or courtship talks or dating advice. There might have been a house rule of not dating until a certain age or not riding in a car with a boy until a certain age, but such didn't apply to me because I didn't have a boyfriend until the summer after my junior year in high school. By then I was turning seventeen.

I learned of the biology of sex from peers when I was about twelve. Once I knew how babies were conceived, I thought it ridiculous that the husband was always surprised when the wife was pregnant on a TV show. I didn't know it was a hit or miss effort. With this knowledge, I now grasped *why* my younger siblings were my half-siblings, and I didn't like it one bit. I'd always thought since we came from the same mother, we were siblings—I didn't like the "half" part. I always knew I had a person called Ralph (or Dad to his face) who I did not share with my younger siblings, but I thought that was only because my mother was married to him at the time of my birth. I was a pretty naïve kid.

The concept of a boyfriend was never up for discussion. On the day of my junior prom, there was a moment, a brief millisecond moment with my mom. My best friends had boyfriends and were going to the prom. I did not have a boyfriend and therefore was not going. Instead, I had yet another babysitting job down the street. I was teary-eyed, and when my mom asked me why, I told her. I recall a moment of gentleness, of her feeling sympathy for me. But the moment passed quickly.

She said, "Look at it this way, you'll be earning money." While I recognized the attempt at a positive spin, babysitting compared to having a date was an apples-to-oranges comparison.

My first boyfriend was eighteen to my seventeen, and we dated for almost two years. Our first time out together was as part of a group of six kids who all hung out at the military base pool in the summer. We were all going to one of those traveling summer carnivals that pop up in strip-mall parking lots. I wore a new pair of grey jeans and a new purple-and-grey top I'd sewn myself—a high-necked halter with a zipper up the back that was far less racy than the popular string-tied halter tops with midriff exposure. The jeans were too long and dragged on the ground, and I wore those flat leather sandals with the leather ring around the big toe. Such was fashionable in 1972. I took the sandals off at some point and carried them. My feet were swollen and sweaty, and the dirt on the ground felt better than sliding in the sandals with the dirt forming mud between the soles of my feet and the sandals.

Out of the blue, I saw my mom, stepfather, and younger sister. While they knew I was going to the carnival, they never told me they would be there too. An hour or so later, the group wanted to go for pizza, and I knew I needed to stop at a pay phone and call for permission. My mom seethed at me over the phone and told me, "You looked like trash." I think she was referring to the jeans dragging on the ground and my bare feet because she'd known what I planned to wear and had complimented my sewing. I wasn't mature enough to even consider challenging the cruelty of her scolding or how humiliated I felt. I mean, really, for crying out loud, what was her purpose?

I was forbidden to go for pizza with the others and told to get home. I had to go back to the car and tell the other five people I had to be taken home. I was "in trouble," and my face probably showed the anxiety I was feeling. Our driver dropped everyone else home first.

When we were alone in the car, he asked, "What did she say?" (Yikes! I was alone in the car with a boy!)

I told him and he responded, "You don't look like trash to me." Then he kissed me. That was it. I had a boyfriend.

It's highly possible my mom's harshness was egged on by my stepfather, but the actual verbal disciplining was placed in her lap. That was the pattern. She was chronically vigilant in attempting to keep my older sister and me above his scorn. Her discipline needed to be sufficiently effective to stunt his annoyance. If it wasn't, his criticism would roll her direction. Her learned behaviors of self-protection, of no one acting superior toward her, simply wouldn't let that happen.

There I go again, letting my mom off the hook. But in years to come, she'd earn my pardon. She'd acknowledge and apologize for such occurrences in the past.

My boyfriend was not "college preparatory"; in fact, he worked in a floor-covering store doing installation labor. This did not sit well with my mother. She never really said anything, though. She never had to. I knew. He was never, not once, made to feel welcome in our house. Conversely, I was openly welcomed in his parents' home. In fact, although he'd had girlfriends before me, they said I was the first girl he ever brought home.

I was not allowed a car for pleasure use, so if we were going to spend an evening at his house, he had to drive forty minutes round trip, twice, to pick me up and bring me home. He barely commented on how unfair my parents were with this rule. This was not because we didn't have a vehicle, as we had three cars sitting in front of our house. This rule was financially based. We were constantly reminded, "Gas is not the only expense in the cost of running a car."

Secondarily, the forbiddance was also a parental control measure regarding any courtship. At his house one evening, they were having steak for dinner and invited me to stay. His sisters, who were my age and younger, set up a small round table with a dark red velvet cloth and a white lacy overlay with two chairs in a separate TV room, just for the two of us. The rest of the family ate in the dining room, and his sisters played waitress, complete with "Monsieur" and "Madame," serving our salad, entrée, and dessert.

I cried through the whole dinner. I wasn't weeping because of how nice it was or how special I felt, although it was nice and I did feel special. I was crying tears of sadness that this would never have happened at my house and that I could never tell of this experience to my mom. She would have had an unreadable reaction, except in its distaste. Maybe she would have been hurt that I was finding joy in my time with a different family, but that wouldn't have lasted.

She would have jumped to anger, angry that his family was actually buoying the relationship of which she was leery.

Once, in his car, I reached for the volume dial on the radio and accidentally cranked the volume too loud. Instinctively, he reached for the dial also, just to turn it down. But I flinched. He looked at me and asked, "Did you think I was going to hit you?" His question caused me awareness of my unconscious reaction. I'd learned to flinch when my stepfather showed a power-trip gesture toward me.

I know I did things I shouldn't have. I know I was falling far short of my mom's expectations. But I had a boyfriend! I had someone who wanted to be with me. I belonged to that elite club among my peers, being part of a couple. I could double-date with my best friends. I had somewhere to go on Friday and Saturday nights and someone to go with! And he was nice to me. He gave me generous gifts for birthdays and Christmas. He gave me an all-in-one stereo record player and a nine-inch black-and-white TV for my bedroom. All of his siblings had their own record players and TVs in their bedrooms, and he was modeling *his* family norms.

My mother sneered, "Boys who give those gifts only want one thing." Little did she know ... that *one* thing was already gone. I didn't and still don't feel I had done something so horrendously wrong. The culture of females was changing. Gloria Steinem and Betty Friedan had brought the women's movement to the forefront. Collectively, we were encouraged to be freer with our choices. Engaging in sexual behavior at age eighteen was the norm within my circle of friends with boyfriends. I was defying her secretively, in keeping with adolescent maturing, and believed her to be out of sync with the times. If I was "cutting the cord" in my relationship with my mom, I thought it was normal. I knew she'd be angry, and I feared her anger, but the want of a boyfriend outweighed my fear.

Once I started community college, a new rule was arbitrarily imposed: I could only see him on weekends. Supposedly the new rule was to keep me focused on my grades, but my grades had never been a problem. I'd been an honor roll student throughout high school, and the semester was just beginning. The reason was just a ruse. The real purpose was to lessen the frequency of our dates. I abided the rule without argument. Starting a new daily life with college and new friends, of which he was not a part, presented changes. I certainly wouldn't have ended our relationship—wouldn't give up the bird in the hand for one in the bush, but he did. Our commonalities were becoming less, and he saw it before I did. Whatever the reason, our time was up.

My mom abhorred snobbery and vowed she'd never impose a superior attitude on others. But when it came to her kids, no one met her expectations. No one passed her litmus tests. Her intolerance of any courtship was spread evenly on all us kids. She was stubborn that way.

Let there be no mistake. While he was not a dummy, he was not a good student and was not college bound. He drove a souped-up Dodge Charger, he liked to work on cars, he liked the drag races, and he smoked. It can be said he ran with a different crowd than I did, a rougher crowd. And he was an eighteen-nineteen-year-old, red-blooded American boy, with a great deal more boyfriend-girlfriend experience than me. Mom's worries had reasonable foundation. However, he was also honest, hardworking, respectful to his parents, caring toward his three younger sisters, kind to me ...

and he *liked* me. The boys in my circle didn't. Once he accused me of envisioning him in the future behind a desk, wearing a suit. He was right, I did, but I wouldn't admit it. I thought we were just teenagers still finding our way, and the "way" that was instilled in me was to go to college and be a professional. I wish my mom could have seen the good in him, though. He treated me nicely, and she would have liked that.

For my college years, I had a couple of short relationships and a high number of dumb liaisons, to put it kindly. I was brash, I was a bartender, it was the middle 1970s, and I was on the pill. Once that barn door is open, it's hard to close it. Promiscuous is a bit of a stretch, but not far from it. Not my finest hour. Influences from the women's movement were up close and out loud. The mantra was to be uninhibited and not prudish. We were brazen and braless. If men slept around, why not women? Sheesh, the seventies were rough!

In retrospect of this time and of years to follow, I can identify significant causes in my relaxed moral decision-making. I felt obligation. Culturally the women's movement was telling me to be engaged in the sexual revolution. Participation was a show of strength, self-confidence, and freedom. Also, I was so over-the-moon when any man graced me with his interest or affection, I believed reciprocation through sex was the expectation. Desire on my end ranked third. Call it a warped quid pro quo. I lacked trust, faith, or confidence in my personality, sense of humor, or simply my presence being of enough value.

I'm quite certain my mom was a "good girl," although the topic was never, ever discussed. *She* didn't have the supposed necessary paternal figure, and I doubt *her* mother offered any more guidance than I'd received. If she ever felt desirable or conscious of feminine wiles, she never exposed it—except with her kitten-heeled slipper request. Therefore, she couldn't teach it by word or by action. Yet she had a rigid self-worth, even if born out of defense. There lies a difference between us that I've yet to name. She developed a self-worth perhaps in defiance of her poverty-stricken childhood.

After college, I left Minnesota in my chartreuse green Opel station wagon and drove east to Chicago. I vowed to turn over a new leaf. I was no longer a college kid. I was an adult with a career and I planned to act responsibly. I had a few dates and a couple sexual encounters. But my expectations had changed. Now I was no longer a student. I had a real job, and I was hoping to find love.

I moved five times in my first five and a half years after college: Chicago (three different apartments), Indianapolis, Cleveland, Denver (for the first time), and back to Chicago. After the first five years, I traveled for fifty to eighty percent of my work. For the next three years, I traveled for assignments of eight to twelve weeks, without a break for a trip home. Not to mention restaurant management is a hefty workweek, and I was an overachiever in work. Developing a personal life was not possible ... or at least not a priority. Finally, when I was transferred back to Chicago and only traveled a consistent thirty percent of the time for five- to ten-day stretches, I was hell-bent to seek balance in my life.

Now, I'm caught up in the story. In the late 1980s, my good friend and I were going to Soldier Field to see a Chicago Bears game. My first professional football game—remember "Da Bears"? Seats were hard to get, as season ticket holders, predominantly men, occupied the majority of the stadium. I was so excited and, of course, called my mom and told her.

So here it is, the *one* piece of relationship-designated, female-behavior advice, thirty-plus years in development, she somewhat timidly offered: "Try to act demure."

Holy crap! What the heck was demure? Webster's dictionary defines it as prim, proper, nice, decent, serious, and silent. If she was telling me how to meet a husband, she was a little late—that ship called *Demure* had already sailed!

I laughed when she said this. First, I thought she lacked awareness of the independent, tough-gal image I often presented. A posture I thought was necessary to work and live as I did, *independently,* even if it was contradictory to seeking a husband. Second, clearly my mom had never been to a Bears game.

My friend and I filled a thermos with hot chocolate and spiked it with peppermint schnapps. We drank a screwdriver in the car on our drive downtown. We even had a refill in the deep pockets of our cargo jackets to smuggle into the stadium (I know, I know, escaped by the skin of my teeth). By the time we reached the parking garage, we could hardly control our laughter at trying to understand how to act "Da mirror." We weren't laughing at my mom. We were laughing at how the advice seemed so absurd to our intent. We were going to a Bears game, not to a social mixer to meet a husband.

There was never a welcome of any courtship in our family home. I'll never know why. After my first young romance, I never brought a romantic interest into our home. Oh, let's not gloss over it—I didn't have one to bring! Finding the spot, the pinhead on which to land, where I could have the attention of a man and

137

maintain my mother's approval, was too difficult. What if he used a swear word in her presence? What if he wasn't competent at playing cards or games—a habitual social activity within our family? What if he didn't accept our abstinence from alcohol in my mother's presence? Or, God forbid, what if he used "lay" instead of "lie"?

I'm kidding—but only a little. All of us adult kids consumed alcohol to some social level, but not in the presence of Mom. This was a choice we made without much discussion between us. Why rock her boat? Wasn't worth the disappointment or pain it would cause her, let alone her perceptible distaste. Incredulous as it sounds, all these things hovered over me. What if she didn't like him, as had been the case in the past? Little by little, I became more and more convinced I would never find love until after she was gone.

Once, I floated this comment to one of my sisters, probably just to see her reaction. If memory serves, I think she nodded without verbal response. Even though maternal love and romantic love aren't on the same playing field, I was afraid to give up the bird in the hand for the bird in the bush. I never said these thoughts to my mom. The assumption or accusation that my being single was somehow her fault would have been blaming or hurtful. Besides, it took me over thirty years of little-by-little thinking to land on this thought. Yes, her influence was planted and my perceptions were unknowingly guided, but my own experiences were equally contributory to romantic lapse, and I accepted the responsibility if change was to occur. Mom softened some over time—a little bit after her second divorce and a little more as my siblings' marriages gained tenure, but the edges were never fully rounded.

When our family gathered and we'd arrange the little kids in sleeping bags and couples in the guest room or on air beds, I was usually relegated to her living room sofa. She'd feel bad about it and say, "Just because you're single, shouldn't mean you don't get a bed or bedroom!"

I replied with false haughtiness, "Yeah, and when I come visit with a man, I'm getting *your* room, married or not!"

She hardly balked; she actually faked solidarity. "Yeah, that's right!" But we both knew such would never happen.

I'LL GRANT YOU MOST

My mother was not the person to offer this reply to my assertion, "All men are assholes." My counselor said it. Most times, there's a risk my mom might have agreed; besides, I wouldn't have used the "a" word in her presence anyway. Counselors or psychologists are similar to chefs and bartenders; they're a dime a dozen. But great ones are worth their weight in gold. I was lucky to find Jane through a referral from an actor-waiter in my employ.

My inner-self unhappiness, not yet fully defined, stemmed from not being happy with me. I thought I'd done life as I was supposed to. I'd gone to school, struck out on my own, worked hard, and achieved career advancement and a degree of financial stability. Yet here I was, halfway through life, with a job that now left me cold and with no prospects for a loving family life.

Professionally, for sixteen years, work had ruled my life and fueled my soul and mind with feelings of value. My supervisors valued me, my peers accepted and partnered with me, and my staffs honored me with hard work and loyalty. Yet, when a failed venture within the company needed a scapegoat, I was chosen. There was no firing, no reprimand, in fact no commentary at all, simply a transfer to a tired, old, doomed-for-closure restaurant assignment.

I no longer felt wanted, needed, and appreciated at work. In fact, I'd felt pushed aside and had done nothing to deserve it. I felt betrayed. Those leaders (all men, except the one human resource woman), in their self-serving incompetence, no longer valued my efforts. The company had not made a profit during my entire tenure. Conversely, I had led in most measurable categories of performance within my specific areas of responsibility. To provide a balanced viewpoint, I did lack sophistication and maturity born of a cultured lifestyle or upbringing, but I more than compensated with my work ethic. Oh, I could go on and on, but that's a whole 'nother story. The point is I was stripped of my self-worth because I'd mistakenly aligned it with career-worth.

Personally, I felt unloved and unlovable, except in my relationship with my mom. There had to be something wrong with me. How come a man never chose me? Why is the choosing theirs anyway? I could answer this with my emphatic statement, "Because all men are assholes."

Lesson one. I tended to polarize my assessments: all or nothing, always or never. Jane laughed when she said, "We're going to change that to 'most.' I'll grant you most."

How come I wasn't married and becoming a mom myself? I was thirty-six years old and wanted to know what decisions I'd made that put me on this unfulfilling path so I could realign or reverse those decisions. With Jane's guidance in my head, I sometimes talk out of both sides of my mouth. The old patterns and judgments pop up on occasion while the counselor-infused thoughts are trying to break through. I'm sure Jane (and Dr. Phil) can pinpoint them all. Counseling is difficult, emotionally draining work, but it's also pure selfish indulgence. I loved it. I can understand how some people can become life-long patients, but that wouldn't be me.

More than a year into the process, I asked her, "When will I be done?"

She replied, "When you start asking yourself the questions I'm asking you."

The ending of my two-year, weekly one-hour sessions, in the privacy of her sunroom, was marked by a job change and geographic move from Chicago to Denver. However, seeking the job change and move were prompted *immeasurably* by the confidence gained in learning to ask myself questions.

Jane told me wellness counseling would not change any *things* in my life, but the awareness gained during those hours would change my perspective on those things. At the time, her comment didn't thrill me. Where was her magic wand? What's the purpose, for crying out loud? But she was right. For example: As a Labrador of loyalty to my company and its leaders, their devaluing of me caused public degradation and self-doubt. Once I viewed the situation through a less self-deprecating prism, my perception of their disregard changed. The need to blame was their weakness, versus my thinking something was wrong or less in me. Furthermore, I have the statistical performance data, pre and post, to qualify my enlightened perspective. This seems so simple, but it wasn't.

Back to the men. Any judgment, assessment, or evaluation

from a man was programmed into my upbringing as "right." The dad was "right" in the household; he wasn't smarter and "righter" than the mom, but he still sat in a slightly higher chair, by nature of gender. Therefore, it's only natural to evolve into thinking the boss was right by nature of his gender. Then it's not a big leap to believe that if men don't have an interest in me, they're right and something, many things, are seriously wrong and undesirable within me. While this synopsis is way oversimplified, I didn't like the power I perceived men to have over my self-image. Most often, when trying to make a change in perspective, the pendulum has to swing in the opposite direction with equal force to eventually come to rest in a reasonable, healthy center.

When meeting with Jane, I'd already thrown the pendulum from loyal as a Labrador (deferring to male superiority, especially in my job) to "all men are assholes" without definitively knowing why, and I was carrying defensive, childish hurt. Throw in sexual abuse, or the feeling of not being chosen by men, and that protective shield was up!

Mom had an internal argument of the same nature. She didn't often share her quandary, and she didn't carry her "women's movement" as a flag. But it festered within her and would boil over in anger when she suffered specific moments of powerlessness. I found a simple note-to-self, perhaps for future writing, in her piles of written work:

Merit is most important – to know that you are a worthwhile person. Sponging off someone is not a definition of a woman who doesn't work outside the home.

*Can love children - but lunching with a pre-schooler for
more than ten years doesn't make for stimulating conversation.*

*Equal rights doesn't mean participating at the
Thursday night out with the boys - who would want to
be part of all the smoking, drinking and loud chewing of
the many delicacies reported to be eaten?*

*Things that women do are of no interest to the
readers, dull, commonplace, and if it could be considered
exciting, the woman is classified as a kook or an oddball.*

These musings were written during the years she and I were
pursuing our undergraduate degrees, the mid-seventies. She never
spoke these words out loud, but her distaste for obligatory cocktail
parties was well known to me. I assumed her dislike was related to
the booze only. Come to find out, with these notes, it was just as
much about the dismissal men projected on women.

The notion of women being smart, self-reliant, and competent
was drilled into me from the life experiences that came before me.
Fannie did it all—earned the money, protected her children, raised
and supported them to the best of her ability—not only without
assistance from her husband but also in spite of his burdensome
presence. In her time, women *were* considered inferior and merit-
less without the husband, regardless of his behaviors.

While Barbara did not work outside the home, she did all
the work inside the home. Her husbands *never* cooked, cleaned,
shopped, or did laundry. Generally, fathers were far less partic-
ipatory in the homemaking and child-nurturing processes than
they have been for subsequent generations. Our home life was no

exception. She supervised vehicle repairs, attended school func-
tions and parent-teacher conferences, checked homework, nursed
illnesses, and chauffeured kids to Little League, piano lessons,
drum lessons, orthodontic appointments—the list is too long to
mention them all.

We moved seven times in eighteen years, across the country, in
and out of the country, and an additional four household moves
within a city. She navigated these moves, settling four kids with
a ten-year span in age into as many as three schools each time.
Yardwork and car washing were the domestic areas in which her
husband engaged, but she was often outside with him, working
side by side.

Sometimes she resented all this responsibility falling her way,
but rarely did she openly expect more from him. Oh, she'd get all
huffy and say she's going on strike and then sulk for a day. He'd
humor *at* her and belittle her, offering no support, and the roles
never changed. Reinforcement continued: the man is right. The
weight of the pressure took a toll, and her patience for our needs
was lost on occasion. She was often dismissive of teenage angst or
the need for one-on-one understanding. Frequent family reloca-
tions presented struggles that were not afforded much credence.
Sometimes, when retelling an event years after the fact, she might
have exposed the little pang of empathy that had been there, behind
her façade. But she relentlessly clung to her reality of our life being
so much better than hers as a child; therefore, complaints were
without merit.

I was learning, overtly and covertly, the strength of independence, of not needing a man to do-for me, as a self-defense

weapon versus a confidence builder. In my late thirties, I was visiting with friends at their home. They were a married couple with a two-and-a-half-year-old son and a six-month-old daughter. I sat at the kitchen table as the husband prepared dinner and completed all the associated cleaning while his wife sat with me at the table, mothering the baby. I was anxious, feeling compelled to abandon the relaxation at the table and help with the dinner chores.

The husband said, "No, you sit, relax; just enjoy visiting." He enjoyed hosting and took pleasure in doing-for. Bears noting, he was a restaurant person, a do-for person.

The wife said, "He's got it; you don't need to help," with a subtle undertone, communicating that he *should* take on such responsibility.

I had never witnessed this display of division of work in my entire life. It was a lightbulb moment. She knew how to be done-for. I started looking for this behavior in other couples I knew. Why was my mother never the recipient of such kindnesses? What was the difference? Probably at least part of the answer is relative to cultural changes. Women's "home" work was beginning to earn more value. But the answer for Mom may be quite simple: she was never done-for by a man or a father, and she'd never witnessed her mother being done-for, so her expectations were no greater from her husband. All of that seeped into my expectations and my evaluations of men. Observing my friend's husband's participation in "home" work put a chink in the armor of my ingrained perceptions. Perhaps the pendulum does have a middle ground, a healthy restful center.

I like to think a gauge of love is found in the ability to see another's faults, not as deal-breakers, but more as characteristics or quirks, even endearingly. I have felt such affection, seeing a person through rose-colored glasses, but I don't know of being on the recipient side. I do expect to be valued for my can-do spirit, my independence, my "whirling dervish of productivity," my gregariousness, and my tendency to do-for. Since only "most" men are unacceptable (assholes), that means there are at least "some" who are exceptionally acceptable. I'll keep looking.

THE WORLD DOES TEND TO REVOLVE IN TWOS

Mom was validating my occasional feelings of loneliness as a young woman, especially when in the presence of couples or on special occasions. While she understood my feelings, she felt quite differently. My mom had two marriages that lasted for about thirty-five years of her adult life. She was completely content and happy with not being married for the last twenty-five years of her life. She was not lonely. She enjoyed so many things about her life and daily activities, including friends, family, church, singing, tap-dancing, working, and occasional travel. She often remarked of her pleasure in the freedom to do what she wanted, when she wanted, without worry to please the wants of a husband. She chose optimism; she chose to be happy.

The world revolving in twos is a fact, be it cultural or even biblical, and single people can often feel like a fifth wheel. I hasten to commend a few wonderful husbands of my friends who have welcomed my presence as a single woman, never expressing any annoyance with the out-of-balance gender count. For my contribution, I'm quite adept at relating to men platonically.

Conversely, when meeting an *available* man (and I can spot the difference a mile away), I used to be overwhelmed with nervousness. I'd put up a protective, impenetrable shield. Quickly. I was convinced my talkativeness, only increased by nervousness, would be viewed as annoying. The volume of my voice would be irritating, exposing gregarious enthusiasm would be cause for rejection, and any excess pounds exacerbated my insecurities. So I'd clam up. My mom could see the shield, even though there may have been only a couple of millisecond instances when she would have observed it.

In those instances, she'd say, "If you'd just act like yourself." But myself was overly protective, preparing for dismissal or perceived judgment from a man. I wasn't conscious of the shield until it was locked in place. Then I'd lament its presence. Fear had top billing: fear of rejection, fear of being duped or dumped.

Oh, the irony of it all! I'd built an adult life being defiant, intolerant, and fearful of men having power over me, only to allow them complete and total control over me in seeking romantic relationship. I'd had instances or beginnings of romances when I tried so hard to be open, tried to be honest with myself and recognize when I'd felt those insecurity triggers of victimhood or powerlessness. I'd tried to power through those triggers versus let them reinforce mistrust. The mildest of rejection felt like a shunning. The mildest of critique felt like a betrayal.

Confusion still lies in expectation.

I've been witness to only a couple of marriages I envy. Oh, I envy parts and pieces, but when I observe arguments or cruel banter, it's distressing. Mom's friends Edna Mae and Lehnis were an exception. My mom often said that Lehnis was one of a kind. He frequently opened the car door for Edna Mae for the sixty-plus years they were together. They held hands when walking down the street. They expressed disappointment with the evolution of bucket seats and mandatory seatbelts so she could no longer sit close to him when riding in the car. If either was telling a story, the other listened intently, as if hearing of the event for the first time. He prepared the coffee pot every evening so it would be ready for him to bring her a cup in the morning. They apologized if one unconsciously interrupted the other, as one would with a new acquaintance. I can assume compromises were made, but they weren't boasted. Common courtesy and appreciation were prevalent.

Married just out of high school, how did they figure it out? How much weight can be placed on perhaps both having witnessed similar marital behaviors from their own parents? I don't know, but I've always wondered. My mom lamented a couple of times her inability to provide that example to us kids. I discovered a handwritten note within her cherished box of writings: *The secret of a happy marriage: Falling in love several times, with the same woman.*

For the first half of my life, I had little or no true perspective on Lehnis. He was the father in a household, the person who went to work every day, the husband of the mother in the house. Being leery of older men, I would never be caught in any room, in any house, alone with a man. If the women momentarily left the living room to, let's say, refill their coffee cup, I joined them. I was uncomfortable in any one-on-one encounter and coped through avoidance. I must have been good at it because the pattern was never detected, even by my mom.

However, in my mid-forties, graced with an intention to break patterns in my perspectives, I saw him differently. He was humble, caring, and comfortable in his own skin when expressing his love for his wife, daughters, grandkids, and his faith. His internal moral compass pointed due north.

Truth be told, there was a conversational exchange between Lehnis and me, which embedded in my heart and contributed to the enlightenment. We were standing in my mom's kitchen, sharing our private thoughts regarding our individual, intangible connection with a specific grandson (his) and a specific nephew (mine). Of course, we both loved all members of our respective next generation equally, but there was no denying these individually unique and reciprocal affections. After a momentary pause, he said, "You were always my favorite of your mother's."

I can't repeat that compliment without tears welling up in my eyes. A man, with no reason or purpose, no agenda, no expectation of anything from me, who had known me all of my forty-seven years to date, albeit with intermittent visitation, had said I was held in high regard. I had no reply. My voice was stymied. I can only hope he knew how I felt in seeing the moisture and gratitude in my eyes. Viewing his strength, humility, and kindnesses through the broader lens of adulthood was an "ah-ha" moment.

When my girlfriends would say, "I need to ask my dad" or "I need to talk to my dad about that," I couldn't relate other than, "I need to talk to my mom." My dad was never, not once, the choice. The impression he provided was that he couldn't be bothered. I do think he felt concern in his heart, but he couldn't openly display caring or nurturing in any way. At six, after my first major oral surgery, I was sitting with a TV tray, trying to slurp warm Jell-O, when he came home from work. He looked at me, then walked on through to the other room without a comment, without a word of compassion or sympathy for a little kid with a swollen, injured, stitched mouth.

When I was molested by his brother-in-law, his one and only gesture was to walk past me and fake-punch me in the upper arm. How can a child build trust and value from that behavior? When he did engage, it was usually with dismissal. As a kid, I was oblivious to any mood or culture in our home. As an adolescent, I became more aware and often felt cautious, not wanting to step out of line or get in trouble, not wanting to be an inconvenience or to risk anger, forever alert for the other shoe to drop. Lehnis was the first adult male, authority, paternal figure with whom I felt trust. He was barely five foot four inches tall to my five-foot-nine-inch height, and I probably outweighed him by thirty-plus pounds, but he was the biggest man I've ever known.

Nearing forty years old, I left Chicago and headed for Denver and a new job, with the seeds of new perspectives planted in my head, garnered from time with Jane. I was determined to throw caution to the wind. I'd spent a couple of years examining past experiences and developing a better, healthier, adult perception of those experiences. I wanted to be open to opportunity, open to expose my feelings, to be less judgmental or harsh toward men, and less harsh toward me. In any event, I was determined to change my patterns of shielded self-defense and how I viewed men or how I thought they viewed me. Changes in these patterns were like trying on new clothes and shoes, a new hairstyle and makeup, all at the same time. Some were too tight, or too long, or too short, or too large, or just not flattering. That hit the nail on the head: not flattering. I made a few mistakes.

My first mistake lasted eighteen months. I met a man who checked off many positives on my list. He had a son, twelve years old. He was very tall and coached in his son's basketball league. He was fun-loving and charismatic. He was also down on his luck in the job department. As the months passed, his bad luck proved to be an omnipresent condition in *all* departments.

At times, he would emotionally break down from the failures in life. He would cry and plead with me to help fix his life. His tears reminded me of my mom's experience of my stepfather similarly expressing a plea for her help. I understood how she could be induced, as feeling needed is a powerful drug. My money earned with my blood, sweat, and tears supported his life, and he liked to live a pretty darn comfortable life. At first I didn't care. So what, it's just money. I let down my guard in expressing my affection and tendency to do-for, totally abandoning the patterns I'd held for years to protect my heart and pride.

The situation continued to spiral, eventually his actions caused me to receive a knock at my door one night with the delivery of a legal document, a summons regarding some con-artist action he'd committed. I didn't want to hurt his son by abandoning the relationship, but a wise friend said, "How's his son going to feel when you put his father in jail? Because that's where this is heading ... he won't stop. His patterns will only escalate."

Those words were a smack-upside-the-head wake-up call.

I changed the locks on my house for the third and final time. What purpose does it serve to mention the first two times, as I ended up giving him a key anyway. Even the thrice-employed locksmith shook his head in disbelief, saying, "Are you going to learn this time?"

I took back the car I was paying for in a middle-of-the-night caper and closed the book. I truly have no regrets, except the money. Lots of money! I was used, I was conned, I was cheated, lied to, and stolen from, and it was definitely not flattering.

Next I met a man with a job. *Check.* Two kids from a previous marriage. *Check.* He owned a home. *Check.* Things were lookin' up! This relationship started as if right out of a Danielle Steel romance novel. The morning after our third date, I called my mom. She happened to be traveling, visiting Edna Mae and Lehnis. As I told her about this new person in my life, I know she heard my excitement, my happiness. I also recall a feeling within myself of waiting for the other shoe to drop. I don't know why I felt that trepidation. Maybe it was foretelling, or maybe it was an old coping mechanism pattern to prepare myself in the event of disappointment. But it was there in the back of my throat behind my excitement.

One of the best feelings I've ever had was one evening when I was meeting him in a high-end restaurant after I'd been on a business trip. I arrived at the restaurant directly from the airport. I tend to walk quickly; I move with purpose. I'm genderless in most personal interactions, especially in my work. I guess my "whirling dervish of productivity" is a chronic condition. I walked in the door of the restaurant and could see him sitting at the bar. The second he saw me, he stood and slightly pulled out the chair next to his, preparing it for me. Call it chivalry or gentlemanly behavior, but that moment stopped me in my tracks.

I silently told myself, "Take it down a notch, lower your voice, move less stridently. Be. A. Girl." Maybe I was telling myself to "act demure." Nah, that's too much of a stretch. But I *was* trying on more new clothes.

This second mistake lasted for eleven years. In the initial few months of dating, I was aware he dated other women. By the end of the first year, unbeknownst to me, he'd chosen to resume a supposedly monogamous relationship with his former girlfriend. He was a cheater, and I was a cheatee. As time passed, I became aware that I was not the *only* cheatee. I'm not proud of my actions. I salve my pride in thinking cheating is different than adultery, and his children weren't involved; he kept them distanced.

All of our encounters were at his beck and call. I had no say, except to say no. I thought about saying no many times, countless times, but when I'd receive his phone call and hear the invitation, I was weak against my inner-self want to feel chosen by a man.

He was also fun, charismatic, and highly gregarious; he had many friends. He also had an underlying attraction to influential people. Don't get me wrong, he was sincere with all of his friends, influential or not, but he definitely coveted prominent people. He was more than reasonably smart and exceptionally quick. Being quick is a necessity when weaving a tangled web of deception. We talked easily, comfortably, in tandem. We played cards and various board games, accompanied with inhibition-reducing intoxicants.

On one occasion, my sisters met him. The youngest said, "He's the male you." There were times when I thought we even looked alike.

One time, when I was out of town on business, he brought the "other woman" into one of the restaurants I supervised. Within a day or so, the bartenders relayed the events to me. Ah, the bartenders; those guys were the best of the best, the cream of the crop, and had the best swagger ever! They had seen me with him previously, and I'd introduced him, but when he came in with another woman, their treatment toward him changed. They told me he was acting "all hooked up" in the restaurant, like he knew somebody important. He did. Me. The service they provided can only be described as barely above the minimum.

I confronted him. My outer self, manager of people, can be a Mother Tiger. "Do you know how difficult it was for my staff to tell me this? Don't ever put them in that position again. You are 'hooked up' in many restaurants in this town. You don't need one of mine."

From then on, when he frequented the restaurant, he was with male friends. Some weeks later, he commented, "I don't think those guys are as good as you think they are," referring to the bartenders.

I couldn't bring myself to tell him the reason for their behavior, although I knew it. Saying the words might sound self-important or might hurt his feelings, so I said nothing. A couple *years* later, he brought it up again, this time with an illuminated perspective on the barely hospitable, borderline condescending service he'd continually received.

"That was about protecting you."

This time I replied, "Yep." Man, I love restaurant people!

What did I think was going to happen? Did I think he'd eventually wise up and choose me? I did, for a while.

Once, maybe during the second year, aware of my "other woman" status and probably trying to hold on to some degree of pride, I said to him, "Don't make me look foolish," but that damage was already done, self-inflicted.

At some point, I listened to the logic in my head versus my emotional want to be liked and knew he would always be a cheater, so I stopped expecting anything to change. But I didn't change either; I still wanted to spend time with him. He certainly was fun, smart, and he liked me! He also was untrustworthy. Sadly, while I was battling internally to keep my harsh, unshakeable, disapproving judgments of men at bay, this pattern risked bringing them back to the surface.

Sometime in the first year or so, my mom gently asked me whether I was still dating him. Since any talk about men or alcohol simply didn't happen, this was the one and only time she asked. I told her that he went back to his former girlfriend, and we were just friends now. My guard was up; my armor effectively hid my disappointment and my half-truth from her. If she saw through it, she didn't let me know.

I did not initiate the ending of the clandestine, secret, closeted relationship. He did. He died. How about that? He had a heart attack and died. I was overwhelmed with sorrow. Regardless of the perversion of this relationship, I had a feeling of being liked, and then it was gone. However, a part of me was glad the relationship was over. For too long, I had been stuck, feeling this was all I could have.

I've had a couple of blind dates. One drove up in a beat-up, rusted-out El Camino car-truck, and he was wearing white sneakers, jeans, a black velour shirt, a large gold-tone chain and medallion, and a flipping mullet! You know, "business in the front, party in the back" hair. It was 2005, but he was lost in the 1980s.

I participated in an evening of speed dating, and I've been a member of two well-known dating websites. All proved fruitless and frustrating. Been there, done that, and got the T-shirt. Not going to happen again. Well, maybe that's an all-or-nothing statement, a little polarized thinking. I'll put a slight *maybe* on that statement.

I seldom feel lonely now, but sporadically I've yearned for that elusive loving, trusting, couplehood relationship. I don't know when my next time in the batter's box will present itself, but I welcome it. My last two swings were surely way outside the strike zone, but I swung away anyway. Perhaps I've gained a more discerning eye and will better evaluate the pitches. Perhaps I've learned to suppress the shield, without abandoning self-respect. Optimism for the unknown is oddly exciting.

Waterbury girls, 1907. "Healthy stock." Fannie, *bottom left*, age 19.

Waterbury girls, 1943. Fannie, *fourth from left*, age 55.

First true home, circa 1946.

June, age 3, 1930. Clothing courtesy of Salvation Army.

Me, age 3, 1958. "Always happy."

June, age 8, 1935.

Me, age 6, 1961. Jack-o-lantern teeth: "A face only a mother could love."

June, high school graduation, 1945.

June, glamour shot, 1947.

A shirtwaist dress 3 days after my birth. "Are you kidding me!?"

Mom and me, 1958.

Fannie, age 70, and me, age 3, 1958.

June and Ralph building a house, circa 1950.

Fannie, age 44, and June, age 5, 1932. "Hard life."

Fannie, age 57, with Henry, circa 1945.

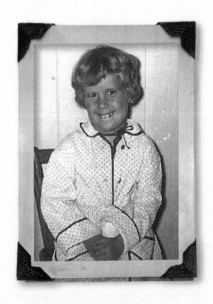

Me, age 4, 1959.

"All that and a bag of chips!" 1984.

The "look" of gratitude.

Great photo! January 1959.

The high school P.L.I.B.S., 1945. *Left:* June.

Mom and me, Christmas 2005.

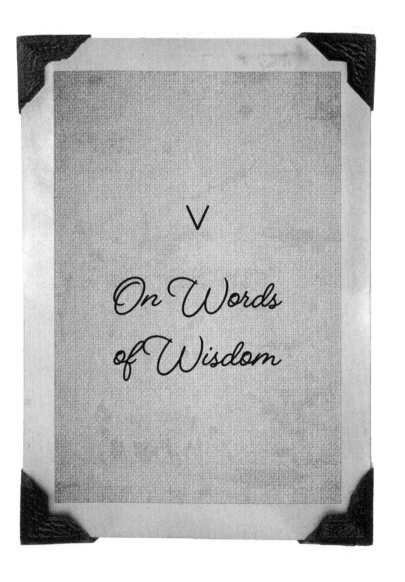

V

On Words
of Wisdom

PAUL MCCARTNEY, who will need no more introduction than his name till the end of *time*, has spoken of a dream about his mother. He was struggling with relationships within The Beatles, and she came to him in a dream and spoke mom words of wisdom, "Let It Be." Three little words gave us a song for the ages.

Mothers model behavior and speak guidance all the time, knowingly or not. Indelible mom quotes. Some are literally famous, like, "Wear clean underwear, you never know when you might get in an accident," or "You're going to poke an eye out with that thing," or the all-time favorite, "Stop crying or I'll give you something to cry about!" Daughters don't always pay attention. When we do, when I did, the words of wisdom took root in my life. She was always teaching.

At least half of the time, Mom's guidance came in good ol' American colloquial phrases. The pot calling the kettle black, two peas in a pod, escaped by the skin of my teeth, treading on thin ice, worked like a man possessed, or to beat the band, par for the course ... and I just love them.

When I was in New Zealand primary school, one of my teachers emphasized penmanship and writing. Almost daily, he assigned us to write a story. Once completed, we would take it to his desk, and he would jot down his feedback. On multiple occasions, he wrote "colloquial" in the margin of my paper, referring to some phrase in my work. I never knew what that meant. As an American kid in the British education system, I was clueless to the critique. These were phrases spoken in my home—I didn't know they had a name.

As I grow older, the managers I supervise grow younger; I'm

old enough to be a parent to most in the group and, to my horror, a grandparent to the youngest. As I lead, guide, or direct their decision-making and business savvy, I've employed numerous phrases garnered from my mother. It's good for a laugh, and it engages their attention. Laughter is relaxing, and we learn better when we're relaxed and engaged. Sometimes an appropriate and well-timed colorful phrase simply hits the nail on the head! The perfect image or feeling is conveyed through the words.

"I was spitting nails!" When Mom was really mad, she'd say, "I was spitting nails!" What a visual! When she was struggling with how to resolve a problem and perhaps spent days agonizing over a solution, she'd say, "I need to stew on that awhile" or the more graphic, "I need to chew (my cud) on that one." I guess that goes back to those gregarious cows.

"You'll never be done!" The month I turned twenty-five, I was promoted to the general manager position at a fairly large, upscale, busy restaurant. I had spent the prior three years in secondary roles in both the service and culinary departments, gaining knowledge, tactical skills, and supervisory skills. I was the youngest general manager ever in the company's history, the fastest ever promoted to the GM position, and the only woman to date. How 'bout them apples? I felt pride and gratitude to all the mentors who'd helped

me learn and all the staff members who'd guided the path before me with their years of experience.

We're programmed with an expectation of scheduled promotions from age five to age twenty-two. Every year, we advance to the next grade in school. Then in college we move from freshman, sophomore, junior, to senior years with the same pattern reinforced. Once in the workforce, I continued with the same expectation. However, once promoted to GM, I thought I'd arrived. This assignment was what I'd been working toward for four years of college and three years in assistant manager and department head positions.

Within a couple months in my position, I made a mistake in handling a situation. Unbeknownst to me, my supervisor was called and informed of the error. Disappointing a supervisor was demoralizing for me. He didn't berate me nor even reprimand me. In hindsight, the error was so minor such reaction would have been unnecessary. He calmly provided direction for me to correct the problem. But I was crushed that I'd made a mistake. I'd worked so hard, I'd worked so relentlessly, I thought I'd gained competence and freedom from making mistakes.

I called my mom. I wailed, "When will I be done? When will I not have to go through this?"

Some mothers might salve the wounds with words of motherly defense or tenderness, such as, "That mean old boss, you are good enough, you are competent."

Not my mom. She said, "Never! You'll never be done. You get to learn and get better for the rest of your life, and when you have kids, you get to struggle through all of their learning too."

I have employed her advice countless times. I suppose that means I've made countless mistakes. And since I have no kids of my own, I've relayed her advice to those who report to me when they are caught in the snares of embarrassment from a mistake or have erroneously thought their journey complete. Wise words.

"Sugar, flour, apples ... what's the problem?" I never cared much for cake and wrinkled my nose at cake frosting. For my birthdays, Mom made pies. My favorite was cherry pie, but I advanced to her lemon chiffon pie in my teen years. A letter for my thirtieth birthday began,

> *Dear Carol,*
>
> *How I wish I could send along a big Lemon Chiffon Pie for your birthday. But, I guess we've both eaten too many Lemon Chiffon pies in the past and that's why we have such a struggle now. Anyway, you can pretend that you are eating a pie - - maybe just remember the pies in the past.*

This letter ended, as all letters did, with a salutation that can render me weepy.

> *Needless to say it's time to wrap this up. Have a really good birthday, and I'm so glad that I will be*

seeing you soon. Thank you for all your help in the wedding (my younger sister's wedding was the prior month) and for all that you mean to me. People who don't have "my Carol" in their lives are missing the greatest and have not lived. I love you.

Mom's pie was a mainstay in our family. One morning, at Mom's house during a family holiday gathering, my niece asked, "Grand'Mere, may I have pie for breakfast?" (With the arrival of her first grandchild, Mom chose to be called by the French word for grandmother.)

My mom replied, "Sure."

I bolted upright in my chair and challenged, "What?"

She said, "Sugar, flour, apples ... what's the problem?"

"The problem is, you never would have said yes to us wanting pie for breakfast when we were kids," I replied.

"Sometimes as a parent, it's just easier to say no to such requests. I'm a grandmother now." She was getting better all the time.

My mom's pie crust is the best. The very best I've ever eaten. Would you believe I'm in possession of my great-grandmother's rolling pin? I asked if I could have it from Mom. I don't know how she had it, although it surely came from Fannie. How did Fannie come into its possession when all her sisters lived in Oklahoma with their mother? It's solid wood, carved with handles; a tool you'd see in a cartoon with a wife ready to bop somebody over the head. I've often thought I could open a successful pie shop using her methods. I love that she taught me how to make her pies. I could hardly wait until I could teach my child to make those pies.

But that opportunity was not to be.

Instead, I've had alternative occasions to teach her technique. I'd befriended a family with four children, the oldest of whom became a professional baseball player. In his teen years, he frequently helped me with heavy yardwork and landscaping projects. One summer while he was a college student, he called to tell me he'd picked a pail of apples and asked if I'd show him how to make a pie for his girlfriend's family. What joy!

We planned to make two pies and mow my lawn while they were baking. I peeled all the apples—they were tiny, and it required at least twelve per pie, double the usual number required. While peeling, I instructed him how to incorporate the ingredients and "cut-in" the dough for the crust. Once the pie was assembled, I was startled by the contrast of watching his large, manly, athlete hands crimp the edges versus the image in my memory of my mom's tiny hands. I also recall, after he rolled the bottom crust and placed it in the pie pan, that tall, strong young man exhaustedly said, "That's just for one?!" And he hadn't even peeled all those apples!

I taught a good friend's daughter how to make both apple and pumpkin pie one Thanksgiving. She suffered through. I became aware that while everyone may like my mom's pie, embracing the heritage of it may be somewhat germane to family ties. Maybe one day she'll appreciate the recipe card with instructions.

And once, two younger women who worked for me came over for a morning of pie-making. It isn't about the filling, as any filling is a personal preference. It's about the flavor, the flakiness, the freshness of the crust. Every time I make a pie, I taste my birthday dessert.

I'm sure you thought I was going to give you the recipe, didn't you? Nope. Not gonna happen. It's mine. But you're invited to my house, anytime, and I'll teach you.

"That's right! And I'm a four-star." One day, someone growing close to our family accused my mom of being a general and of raising four generals. She heard the accusation as the criticism it was, but rather than expose the vulnerability of hurt feelings, she leapt to defensive attack in saying, "That's right! And I'm a four-star."

She did raise four generals. All of us exhibit head-of-household behavior; we're all decision-makers, and we've all endured accusations of "running ramshod" over others on occasion. Furthermore, we all have to guard against the trigger to leap to defensive attack when we suspect criticism.

About a year ago, my youngest niece expressed interest in reading this material. I provided her a thumb-drive copy. I wanted to at least *seem* like I possessed more current technological skills. The truth is I'm a "pencil and paper" gal. The lead is my enter key, the eraser my delete key, and the sharpener is my recalibrate or reboot function.

The year passed without word or comment. Infrequently, I wondered if she had read it but just didn't offer comment, or if she'd forgotten. Now I've come to know she just didn't find the time, as she was in the throes of adding a fifth credentialed acronym after her name while building her practice as a physical therapist. She's also a wife and mother of two small children. Talk about a whirling dervish of productivity!

Unfortunately, we don't communicate with any regularity. Letter writing is becoming an ancient art, with email only holding court for a couple of decades. With respect to my treasure trove of letters, this loss is such a shame. After the year passed, I was surprised by her spontaneous and joyful text message as she neared the midway point in reading. I was glad but had to concede this was her lineage also, albeit from Mom's genetic line through my brother, her father. The next morning her email arrived—a full email-letter. She expressed her wonder, her joy, her emotion, and her awakening to behaviors and patterns she received from those who came before her.

She ended her note with "the piano is my favorite, most meaningful earthly possession. The girls and (her husband) hear from 'the General' if they ever so much as try to set a drink on it. I play it often and think of Grand'Mere—and you, every time."

Whoop, there it is! A fourth generation of the rank. She may need to add another acronym after her name.

"Rip it out and do it again." In home economics class in sixth or seventh grade, we were learning to sew. Simple project: just straight stitching with a rectangular-shaped apron and a casing at the top to run a belt through to gather it at the waist. My mom was a competent seamstress, so when I brought home my work-in-progress, and she saw my crooked sewing lines (of which I was completely unaware), she made me rip out the seams. I thought she was angry

about my poor work. I thought she was punishing me, somewhat for nothing, as the teacher said it was fine and didn't make me rip it out and do it again.

Years later, when Mom was telling the story, she included her judgment that the teacher only paid attention to the students who already had sewing experience, doting on their more complicated project work, while the novice was basically ignored and not taught well. Hmm ...? I never knew she was mad at the teacher versus mad at me, as she would not have given me any opinion to discredit a teacher. Now I know a crooked seam when I see one. And I'm a proficient seam-ripper!

"Give it a lick and a promise." As kids, we had the usual assigned household chores during the school year, like bathroom-cleaning, dishwashing, laundry-folding, and bed-making, but Mom was a true believer of group cleaning over summer vacation. She'd say, "If we *all* clean first, then we *all* get to have fun in the afternoon." While I had little interest in *her* having fun during *my* summer vacation, she was the higher-ranking general.

One particular day we were all in the throes of housecleaning, and she said, "Well, we'll give it a lick and a promise."

Always intrigued by these comments, I asked, "What does *that* mean?"

She replied, "Well, if I told you to go wash your face and maybe you just licked the crumbs from your lips, you'd be giving it a lick and a promise to do better next time."

She taught me to be a pretty good housekeeper, but I'm not averse to licking the crumbs on occasion.

"I want you to know ..." We had been in a foreign country for three years when I was eight to eleven years old. It was the mid-1960s. The United States was in the throes of the Civil Rights events and the Vietnam conflict. As a "yank" kid, mainstreamed into the local school system, the weight of all-American ills seemed to be placed on my shoulders. I was a darn kid! I knew nothing about such things. My mom never allowed us to argue or even engage. We were guests in a foreign country and were expected to act like guests in someone's home. However, she also had her national pride. She'd say, "You're from the best country in the world. You never have to say it. Just know it."

I faced specific attacks from local kids regarding the race riots in the United States. While I didn't know it at the time, our host country's aboriginal people were rejected from mainstream society and only recognized for their cultural entertainment value. Maoris were not welcome in the public areas, and Maori children were not allowed to attend public school. I absorbed nasty, anti-American comments from other schoolchildren on occasion, and my mom never provided me with responses or counters. Truthfully, I wasn't mature enough to process such information anyway.

The day we were leaving the country, standing on the tarmac waiting to walk up the stairs into the airplane, Mom leaned down and said to me, "I want you to know they don't allow the American black servicemen off the base. They don't want them mingling with local women."

I don't know why she chose that time, that place, to say that. Perhaps she had harbored frustration for three years and had withheld the verbal ammunition to fight back. Perhaps there was a black serviceman on the tarmac, and it just popped into her head. But I remember it. I also know this was a time and place in that country's history; much has changed since then. Years later, I relayed this exchange to her, and she had no memory of it. Odd, as it's so clear in my memory.

She wasn't free of bias, maybe no one is, but her bias was evenly spread toward anyone at the far ends of her linear view. She was always excited to meet a dignitary or accomplished individual but was intolerant of boorish snobs. Conversely, she had no softness for people who did not apply themselves to education, good grammar, hard work, and personal responsibility. I can safely assume she learned of these tolerances and intolerances from Fannie and then passed them on to me.

"He can wear his flip-flops, because we live in California." When I was six or seven, I was allowed to buy my first Barbie doll with my own allowance and gift monies I'd saved. Barbies had been introduced earlier with a ponytail hairstyle. Now, the new "bubble-cut" Barbie was on the market, and that's the one I wanted. Back then, in the 1960s, the dolls were purchased wearing just their bathing suit and pool-style shoes. Store-bought additional clothing was rarely

permitted. Instead, Mom would sew clothing for the doll. For my birthday that same year, I was gifted a Ken doll: Barbie's boyfriend.

One day, shortly after my birthday, I was upset because Ken didn't have any clothes; all he had was his bathing trunks. Mom whipped out her sewing machine and fabric remnants and made him a white shirt, complete with a front placket with two snaps disguised with two exterior buttons that looked like gigantic adornments on the tiny shirt, and a pair of brown slacks that were hemmed a wee bit too short. Then she said, "He can wear his flip-flops, because we live in California." Made sense to me!

What a gesture of immediate attention to my wants! What skill, what can-do spirit, what get-it-done behavior to resolve a problem. Mom graced all of her kids with that same spirit. Fannie had graced her with the same "whirling dervish of productivity."

"Too-ra-loo-ra-loo-ra, that's an Irish lullaby." Although I knew she could sing well, I usually only heard her singing when she played a couple of specific songs on the piano and sang or when we sang Christmas carols. The exception was the Irish lullaby. She sang it to my baby sister while sitting in a rocking chair trying to soothe her. I was only eight years old by the time the baby was one, but I can visualize the scene as clearly as if it were yesterday. And I can hear my mother's voice in my head, clear as a bell, a cappella, perfect pitch.

Rarely were we left in the care of a babysitter, as my parents didn't have nor spend money for personal entertainment. However, when they needed to attend an event, an outsider was in charge. One particular lady was much older than my parents, and she was letting my baby sister cry herself to sleep. I was fit to be tied. I glared at that woman as she sat in the rocking chair while we all watched the television, unable to ignore the crying from the bedroom.

Had I been a rebellious kid, I would have carried my little sister into the living room and told that old gal to get up from the rocker so I could sit and soothe the baby while singing Too-ra. But I was too afraid. Afraid I'd be in trouble for defying an adult, afraid my singing couldn't calm my sister and I'd have to eat humble pie. That was a bad evening for me. I know I told my mom about the crying and the sitter's lapse in care. We never had that sitter again. They found a sixteen-year-old neighbor girl, who related well to my older sister, gave my brother and me ankle pull rides around the linoleum kitchen floor, and the baby didn't cry.

Years later when babysitting, I sang Too-ra to many a crying baby. Unfortunately, I did not inherit my mother's voice. I might have, but two thirteen-year stints addicted to smoking sabotaged any hope. My voice is low in pitch and gravelly; at best, an off-key Cher impression. In church, I enjoy the worship songs but leave the singing to those who can. My pooch is the only thing with a heartbeat privy to my singing voice and dancing rhythm, and she's sworn to secrecy.

Mom sang in church, with Lehnis as the baritone and she, the soprano. As a young divorcee, she would place my sister and me in the front pew and tell us to behave and sit quietly. We were four and one years old, respectively, but I guess we did as we were told. One Sunday, Mom and Lehnis were singing a hymn akin to a lullaby.

Edna Mae and Lehnis told me of the story. I climbed down from the pew and crawled up the steps of the church alter, headed for my mom. She bent down, picked me up, and kept singing—never missing a cue.

I have a substantial capacity for memory. My older sister, when struggling to recall a specific incident in our family life, has said, "Let's ask Carol. She'll tell us what we were *wearing* that day." I sure wish I could remember that Sunday morning.

"It's called a shrub." I was thirty years old and had recently purchased a residence with a yard. Prior to that, I had owned a townhome that did not require outdoor maintenance. I needed to learn about yardwork. First, I needed to purchase a lawnmower and learn how to operate it. Mom had no interest or experience in the hobby of gardening but was always a competent hard worker, be it housework or yardwork. She could operate a lawnmower but was always leery of the dangers, and I don't think any of us were taught much about them, even my brother. I headed to a chain hardware store to seek information and purchase the machine. While a big-box store might have been less expensive, I was seeking the individualized service I hoped to receive from a specialized retailer.

The salesman was an older guy, easily in his late sixties. I probably asked questions that seemed ignorant to his life experience, and he was not very helpful. Since I'd learned the lesson of not letting any man treat me condescendingly, I was prepared with a counterattack. I looked at him square in the eyes and said, "Do you know how to operate a sewing machine?" He balked and replied with a simple "No."

Then I said, "Well, I don't know how to operate a lawnmower. I'm not dumb, I just need information. In exchange, I'll buy the mower."

But the taste in my mouth had turned sour. I left the store and headed to a big-box retailer. The salesperson was a teenage boy. I asked the questions I needed to ask, and he provided the answers graciously. He must've had a great mom.

I bought the mower, but little did I know, the machine came in a box and required assembly once I got it home. Ugh! I was outside in ninety-five-degree heat and humidity, using what few tools I owned, attempting to accomplish the task. I did have to go in the house and make a phone call to the store for clarification of the directions, but I got it done. And then I called my mom to boast of my feat.

My following day off from work, I decided to purchase and plant a bush. Our family had never lived anywhere longer than two to three years; we'd never planted a tree and we'd certainly never seen trees grow to maturity over a lengthy time span. I got it done, then called my mom to tell of my accomplishment. She said, "It's called a shrub." Always teaching, she was.

"Oh, isn't that nice!" When Mom visited me as a young adult, I could always depend on her enthusiasm, her delight and appreciation of the most insignificant things. No matter what clothing I wore, she'd say, "Is that new? That's nice!"

This went on for decades. Repeatedly, I'd implore, "Let's just assume everything I wear is new. You never have to ask." But she never stopped asking. I bemoaned her endless appreciation of the smallest, dumbest, most meaningless things, but the impact of her optimism carries momentous weight.

Regardless of my residential surroundings, she was complimentary of everything. My first apartment was plain and meager, and my decorating skills and pocketbook were equally limited. Before leaving the family home in Minnesota, I asked if I could take an old, unused box spring and mattress that were stored in the basement. I also asked if I could have an old sofa, abandoned by the previous homeowners and also stored in the utility area of the basement. Permission granted: I had a bed (on the floor, as I didn't have a bed frame), and a sofa, circa 1950. The sofa was made of nylon bumpy-textured fabric in a faded red color. I mean, I'm talking ugly, with a capital "U"! The back could drop down to make an uncomfortable, almost flat surface for sleeping, with a center crevice between the two parts. I also had a forty-dollar dresser, purchased from a thrift store, and a couple of other small things. The charge to transport my so-called furniture from Minnesota to Chicago was five hundred and sixty dollars, which I did not have. The plan was to reimburse my parents with installment payments once I was settled in my new job.

I found my first apartment in Wheeling, Illinois—a second story, one bedroom. I purchased the least expensive curtains I could find, at the least expensive discount store. The weave of the fabric was barely more than fish-netting. I had two towels and two washcloths and a shower curtain, also from the cheapie store. My college graduation gift was dishes for four, a couple of dishtowels, and a manual typewriter. I think my mom was guaranteeing I'd write her letters. Besides, she had an affinity for office supplies.

One Christmas, when I was sixteen, all of us received the gift of a tape dispenser, complete with a refill roll of Scotch tape, in our stockings. Go ahead, I dare you, try and look excited about that! Three of those four dispensers are still in use today. One, my brother's, took a swan dive off his desk at the hands of his grandson and cracked, spilling the sand from the weighted bottom. But he still has a shoebox filled with tape refill rolls received in his stocking for thirty years. But I digress ... back to the story.

I owned a bookshelf and a toy-chest-style storage box I'd purchased and painted yellow when in high school. Placing the bookshelf on its side allowed a place for my nine-inch black-and-white TV (yes, the same one my boyfriend bought me five years prior), my stereo, and my albums. The toy chest was my coffee table. My co-workers at the Ramada Inn gave me a parting gift of a kitchen trash can, loaded with supplies they'd raided from the motel storage area: toilet paper, tissue, cleaning supplies. That was it. Measly is an understatement!

My parents and younger sister came to visit sometime in those first few months. My mom came through the door spewing complimentary words. "Oh, this is so nice!" "Oh, that looks so good!" "Oh, isn't that nice!?" I don't know how she did it. She was quite simply proud of me. Proud I had my first place, my own place, independently supporting myself, and that's all she saw.

For Christmas five months later, after only a few fifty-dollar installments, she sent me the ledger of my moving debt with a handwritten note across the page, "Paid in full." I'm guessing all those quarters in the Denny's pay phone just to hear her voice, all the times I called to cry about how hard I was working and how lonely I was, all those times I didn't have two nickels to rub together, not to mention the four days I suffered a two-o'clock-in-the-morning Peeping Tom gazing through my fishnet curtains from the cab of a construction vehicle, complete with advice from the local police to "get a weapon"—well, they just got the better of her. She would never have acknowledged that I was living like a pauper; I don't think she ever even thought I was. My poor-as-a-church-mouse lifestyle was more than she'd had at my age, that's for sure.

Conversely, my biological father also visited. I was twenty-two and had not seen him since I was twelve. He and his wife slept and showered in their camper in the parking lot. They stayed for two days. When it was time for them to leave, he handed me fifty dollars and whined sympathetically, "You need a lot of things."

Where was he when I *needed* college tuition, or a car, or braces, or extensive oral surgery, or the countless *wants* of adolescence? Hadn't I just provided an expensive dinner at my place of work, one of the best restaurants in swanky Northbrook, courtesy of my dining benefit?

I'd seen the check a few times, the child support check. The amount was sixty-six dollars a month for both me and my older sister. It never changed—she never asked for more. I'm not sure when it stopped, such things were never discussed. It was a strange feeling to see a dollar amount attributed to your existence—in this case, thirty-three dollars a month. Bears confessing, I wasn't receptive to any advice or input from him anyway, but I thanked him for the fifty bucks.

What a contrast! My mom viewed my newly independent adulthood with optimism and pride, only seeing the good. While I'd learn later how the deficiencies, the shortcomings, my loneliness, fears, and stresses cut her like a knife, she never let on. Conversely, my father let me know, or at least he confirmed, that I was a have-not.

That same Christmas, she sewed curtains for my apartment bedroom window and a coordinating blanket-coverlet and bedskirt. She used four-inch square scraps and remnants of fabric from the many clothes she'd sewn through the years to make a patchwork quilted bed-topper. I still didn't have a bed frame, but I saved the thirty dollars necessary and bought one, so I could make use of the bedskirt. I loved it. I still have that blanket.

We didn't know what a wing-chair was, or a Persian rug, or *anything* about style choices in clothing or décor. When we were teenagers, I don't recall any support of our efforts to learn nor of our decisions. Acquiring style knowledge was a nice-to-have versus a need-to-have, and she didn't have the time or money to be interested. We weren't even taught how to use makeup except to be told, "Go wash your face, you look like a clown!" Sardonically, she later became a Mary Kay beauty consultant, and we became her first requisite customers.

Something changed as each of us graduated into adulthood. She became a cheerleader, a champion for all of us, and expressed compliments toward everything we did. I hope I learned that lesson well.

As my income level grew, my lifestyle and surroundings improved. I had years of debt and years of trial and error in decorating and clothing choices, and "I'll never be done." I am still learning. But my mom only saw "Isn't that nice!" Always.

"You can't expect people to be more than who they are." The other day, I read a posting: "I hate when I plan a conversation in my head and the other person doesn't follow the damn script." The truth of the statement struck me comically. Projection is the counseling word for some of our expectations of others. We attribute our own feelings to others and struggle to understand why people don't react or respond as we would in given situations.

In one instance, I was discouraged with the lack of reciprocation or participation from a person close to me and, as always, chose to discuss this with my mom. After exhausting the thoughts of whys or how comes, she said, "You can't expect people to be more than who they are." Perhaps the gentler word would be "different" than who they are versus "more," but she said "more." I don't know why she was feeling so kindly that particular day, as her comment surprised me. I wonder what she was thinking. In hindsight, her guidance might have come from the counselor she met with for a short time while processing the pain of her second divorce.

My response to being "done-for" is downright lousy, probably a disappointment to others. I feel uncomfortable when someone is doing-for me. Oh, I'm grateful and can say the heartfelt words, but I still feel a bit strange when in the recipient role. I probably don't project the response they are seeking. Either I need to work on that or tell them what my mom told me.

"Another dam project!" My older sister gifted herself, Mom, and me coffee mugs. On the outside of the mug was a drawing of a beaver and the phrase "Another dam project!" We were always in project mode, long before television shows and websites promoted do-it-yourself. Fannie did-it-herself, Mom did-it-herself, and we were following suit. That's how we roll. My sister and I would visit Mom, individually or together, and always attack some planned project. However, early in our adulthood, she brought her skills and can-do spirit to us as we pinched the pennies in our home-making. Mom helped me prepare and execute my first garage sale, and she despised garage sales. Having spent her first twenty years making-do with charity goods, she had an aversion to someone else's castoffs.

She helped me paint the living room in the second home I purchased. It was the first room I'd ever painted. She taught me the technique with cutting-in the corners and how to use a roller efficiently. We both reveled in the simple beauty and transformation created by a couple of cans of paint and a little elbow grease. I can't paint a room today without thinking of my mom working beside me and laughing when I bent over to load the roller with paint and accidentally scraped my hair through the wet wall. I do it every time! My hairdresser asks, "Been doing a little painting?" I've taken to wearing a shower cap when I paint.

"I'll help you; we'll get it done." Sewing a new item is 180 degrees different than mending or altering, and we both detested the latter. I have a box full of fifteen-plus articles of clothing in my sewing closet today, waiting for the burst of inspiration and patience needed to attack the work.

On occasion we engaged in a sewing project together, but that wasn't as often as you'd think. Sewing is a one-person effort unless the other person is happy with only ripping out seam errors and pressing. However, one occasion was the exception. Prior to this particular visit, I'd lost a good amount of weight, enough to drop from the "big girl" stores to a size ten in skirts and pants. She was coming for a visit, and mending was high on the to-do list for the visit. I did the ripping out and pressing while Mom resewed all the side seams, waistbands, crotches, linings, and zippers. I actually let out a giggle of glee when I could hang a skirt on a clip-hanger and the sides were well within the total width of the hanger. My mom giggled too, so happy that I was happy and so glad she could share in the joy of my accomplishment.

My hands look nothing like hers. Actually, I like to imagine my hands may look like my grandmother's, as her rings fit me perfectly. But sometimes when I sew, I see my mom's hands in my mind's eye as I guide the fabric under the presser-foot.

"I'm sorry there are so few photos of you as a baby. It just wasn't a good time." Awareness of more subtle teaching and unconscious learning rang true when I approached my fiftieth birthday. Mom was seventy-eight, and she gifted me a photo scrapbook with a few black-and-white, three-inch-square photos, a few pieces of schoolwork memorabilia, and a number of childhood, adolescent, and adulthood photos. Upon receipt of the gift, I called to thank her.

She apologized for so few photos of me as a baby. There were only four, and only one was of me and her. I'd never noticed the void of photos. The same absence would apply to my older sister while she was three to five and a half years old. It *was* a bad time. Mom was newly divorced, scrimping pennies, and working full-time. Once remarried and my brother was born, she had a thirty-five-millimeter camera and an eight-millimeter movie camera, and our lives were well documented in prints, slides, and silent home movies.

She'd always treated me, and I'd always viewed myself, as part of a family—part of a group of four kids within the family. With numerous photos of all us kids after my brother was born, I'd never noticed the prior sparseness. The lack of photos of just me in early life had been insignificant.

She was nauseated by any behavior reflecting conceit, thinking of one's self as cute or special. Self-centeredness or cutesy behavior was not tolerated. She scolded us if she caught us looking at ourselves in the mirror. All of us grew up lacking balanced confidence, so her methods backfired a bit. We were not indulged with much individualized, special treatment. We were four kids: "The Girls" referenced my older sister and me, "The Kids" referenced my two younger siblings. My older sister endured the role of being the oldest, often the trial-and-error child. My brother, as the only boy, received different stuff or attention because of his gender. The youngest simply lived with us almost like an angel.

She'd taught and I'd learned to be part of a group, to be a team player. At age fifty, I liked realizing that I'd always thought of myself as one of my mother's four children, no less and no more than any of the others. Countless photos or lack of photos didn't change that. But I am my mother's daughter. Armed with her confession of the photographic gaping hole in documenting my early life, I occasionally teased her, playing the violin pity-party.

"Aww, they'd get you under a streetlamp and let you go anyway." When I was about thirteen, my best friend lived two houses down the street, and those two houses were separated by a cross street. If we'd spent an evening at either home and one of us had to walk home after dark, we'd walk together to the midpoint of the cross street and then we'd both run the half distance to our own house. Frankly, we were scared but really didn't know of what.

Mom must have overheard our ritual, and she said, "Aww, they'd get you under a streetlamp and let you go anyway." I giggled at the time. I thought my mom's comment was funny, cool, and her dismissal of frightening thoughts showed bravado.

As my appearance-confidence waned in my teens, I also thought, "My mom doesn't think I look good enough, even for the boogie-man." I suspect she'd heard that phrase from Fannie. I suspect Fannie was teaching her to be brave in avoiding all the predators that had come their way. Today, I believe my mom was teaching me to not live my life in fear. Be aware of your surroundings, but don't be fearful.

"That takes the cake!" All of Mom's kids were schooled in a variety of her activities. Not so much by tutelage, but more by observing her. My older sister and I absorbed sewing; my younger sister took up knitting. She approached the work just like my mom had: no real teaching, no training, just pick up the needles and yarn and figure it out. Engaging in the technicalities was no different than how she approached repairing her bicycle pedal. It was there and needed to be done. Each of us has paid the price of time invested or money lost when we ventured into unknown territory, but we learned and made corrections for the next project. Regardless of the activity, we learned how confidently Mom approached things, and it was ingrained in our modus operandi. Although her teaching was far from a classroom-style, if we showed interest, she offered information.

At Christmastime when I was young, a few wrapped presents would appear under the tree each day during the couple weeks prior to the holiday morning. Maybe one for each of us or maybe just one, but we checked for new gifts under the tree when we came home from school or awoke in the morning. Each of us continued some version of this ritual.

I recall from age seven to perhaps twelve, I would have my turn with Mom in her bedroom for one evening. She'd show me two or three options from which I could select gifts for my siblings. She taught me how to gift wrap, how to put my finger *right there,* with pressure so she could tie the bow. I never could zzziiiippppp the ribbon, though. Then I'd get to come out of her bedroom and place the wrapped gifts at the base of the tree while the others looked for their names on packages. She was teaching the joy in giving. Once I began babysitting to earn my own spending money, when I could make my own purchases and keep my own secrets, the process stopped.

She'd never had siblings at home when she was young. Forget about the siblings; she'd never had a Christmas with numerous gifts under a tree! I wonder how she learned. Perhaps she'd watched a scene in a movie and was intent to replicate the image. Perhaps Fannie did buy her trinkets or socks and underwear for Christmas, even if they were Salvation Army purchases. Socks and underwear were staples, much to our dislike. When my first niece and nephew were old enough, I took them shopping and reenacted the same concept of gift selection, private bedroom wrapping, and the joy in placing the secret gifts under the tree.

Every family has their traditions, their customs, their patterns handed down, generation to generation. One funny reminder of our unconscious repetition of Mom's methods occurred with my brother. Christmas morning, we would be surprised by one or two additional gifts left by Santa Claus. If the gift was large, such as a bicycle or a baby-doll stroller, a larger tag would be tied to the handle with our name and "from Santa."

Early in his parenting years, my brother and his wife unconsciously carried out the same procedure. Well, unconsciously for my brother, anyway. His wife chose to take direction from "the general" at these times. While he assembled a bicycle, he asked her to write the tag on a good-sized piece of cardboard. She followed orders, only to be met by the criticism, "Santa doesn't write like that!" His subconscious vision of our mom's Santa-esque penmanship was inarguable.

Hearing the story, I chuckled and thought, "Oh, really? How *does* Santa write?" I also felt a bond with him regarding the indelible influence our mom implanted. Mom laughed and said, "That takes the cake!"

"You'd get more bees with honey ... And, I'm not kiddin'."
Through my early career-building years, a lack of confidence appeared as a defensive shell. I was fearful of being taken advantage of, being cheated or scammed, or making a mistake, and I was vigilant against these fears. I also confused my want of independence, to be free from the controls of others, with ignorant self-sufficiency: the ability to do everything by myself with the delusion of not needing help. Sometimes my defensive behavior could appear outwardly offensive.

Mom and I were shopping in a large retail store, sourcing materials and supplies for a home project she wanted me to complete while visiting. As usual, we were under the gun. There was a time crunch, and patience is not my strong suit. In fact, my lack of patience may be my greatest shortcoming.

I was conversing with a salesperson, displaying impatience, annoyance, and probably a tiny bit of exasperation toward the hourly staff member. Didn't he know I was pressed for time, didn't he know I was stressed, didn't he know I was trying to get something done *for my mom*!? No, he didn't.

Once we were outside of the store, Mom said, "If you think you're going to find clerks in a store who can relate to your speed and level of communication, you're going to be disappointed, a lot! If they could, they'd be in your job. You'd get more bees with honey."

Well, I know she was right, but this was *almost* a case for "physician, heal thyself." Mom was frequently annoyed with inadequate services or products, but unlike me, she rarely displayed her annoyance directly at a salesperson. Instead, she vented her frustration in saying, "I'm going to write a letter to that company!" And just for good measure, she added an emphatic, "And, I'm not kiddin'!"

I believe she wrote a few letters of this nature, although not as many as she threatened. Her tag of "And, I'm not kiddin'" grew more frequent as she aged, so much so it was funny, at least to the rest of us. Her annoyance grew more intense in the last few years of her life, as her ability to comprehend concepts and technological language diminished. I've heard that we see our own worst faults in others. Even though she didn't recognize her own behaviors in mine, she was no less right. Not a week goes by without the need to remind myself to be patient and kind within an interaction.

I'll always work or behave with expediency; I have a keen sense of urgency and avoid wasting time or energy. Remember, she taught me that whirling dervish of productivity. However, chronically being in a hurry and imposing that hurry on others crosses the line. Mom and I are still working on that.

"'Sleep on it' is very much like 'stew on that awhile.'" The difference is that the subconscious is employed. When I struggled with organizing the order of steps in a sewing project, or how to plan and build some carpentry, or anything with a step-by-step process or to-do list, Mom would say, "Well, you need to go to bed and sleep on it. The subconscious solves problems in our sleep. You'll figure it out."

Darned if she wasn't right! We've also heard it said, "When you're *not* thinking about a problem is the exact time the solution pops into your head." My brain, my subconscious, is overpowering to my conscious in times of intense stress or problem-solving.

When my boss said, "You're being transferred to Chicago ... you need to report next Monday," I could feel a void invade my consciousness. I went home that evening, maybe at five o'clock, and immediately, uncontrollably fell asleep. My body and conscious brain simply turned off. In the morning, I woke with all the steps required to facilitate the move, in perfect chronological order in my thoughts.

A few times in my adolescence, fainting had been one of my coping patterns for extreme stress. As if my subconscious said,

"You don't get a choice. You don't get a say. I'm taking over." I fainted once as an eight-year-old when Mom was tying my Brownie uniform necktie, but that was just because I forgot to breathe. I know it scared her a bit, but I felt oddly complacent about it. I'd fainted. I never knew anyone who'd fainted and had only seen it on television shows.

This loss of consciousness next occurred when Mom questioned me about being with a boy: about where I was and what we were doing. Boom! Down I went. Talk about an admission of guilt! My conscious brain shut down under the stress of the interrogation, and my subconscious took over. The second time she questioned me: Boom! Dropped like a rock!

By the third time, she'd caught on to my "need to sleep on it," and while asking the question regarding my whereabouts and activities, she added, "*And don't you faint!*" It wasn't funny then, but it is now, forty-some years later.

Words of wisdom from Mom, aka Grand'Mere, aka the old grey mare, when I was teasing her. She had a million of them. And now they're mine.

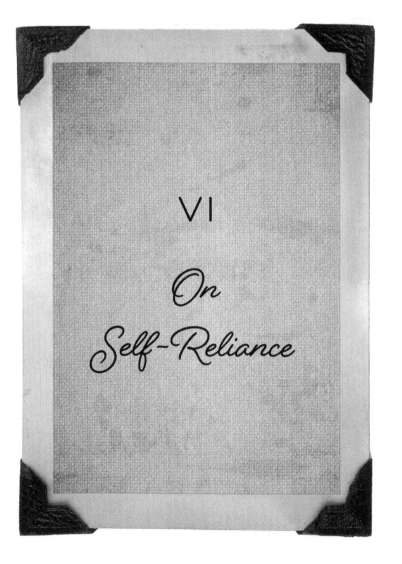

VI

On

Self-Reliance

MOM, ROLL UP THE WINDOW!

My mom's passion for driving a car was life-long. Young women weren't chomping at the bit to get behind the wheel of a car in the early 1940s. In fact, many women of her generation didn't drive until well into adulthood. I grew up with a couple of friends whose mothers didn't drive, even in the 1960s.

She was a good driver, often boasting of her solid, accident-free driving record. When we arrived in New Zealand, our left-side drive Volkswagen beetle was shipped with us. They purchased a second car for Mom's use. It was a 1938 Morris. We called it "the bomb." It was thirty years old, dark green, with two doors, and the right-hand driving position. To crawl into the back, the entire front seat had to be tilted forward, versus just the back of the front seat. Once in the back seat, a kid couldn't even see out of the window—I don't think an adult could either, it was so deep.

During our first weeks in New Zealand, driving on the opposite side of the road, Mom was hit from behind by another vehicle. The blow knocked her glasses off her face and threw my younger brother and napping sister off the back seat. She had to go before the local magistrate so he could hear both sides. Without any child-care available, my younger siblings had to go with her. Being in a foreign country, new to driving on the wrong side of the road, I'll bet she was nervous. She also knew her American accent would stand out like a sore thumb. The magistrate listened to both sides, and the other driver insisted Mom was paying more attention to the kids in her car than the road.

The magistrate replied, "I would be too!"

He found the other driver responsible for the accident. Mom

was vindicated. Had the judgment gone the other direction, we would have heard a different story, for years!

When the family was relocated within the continental US, we moved by car, sometimes one car, sometimes two cars, and once a caravan of three cars. Our vacations were predominantly road trips to visit friends or relatives. Once, all six of us drove in the middle of summer from Southern California to Nebraska in the black Volkswagen beetle with no air conditioning, and drove home with my obese step-grandmother in the front passenger seat. Mom, my sisters, and I were in the back seat with the youngest still a baby, complete with soiled cloth diapers in a plastic bag at my feet. My brother crouched in the way-back, right above the car engine. We must have looked like twenty circus clowns crawling out of a tiny car, when we stopped for gas and restroom facilities.

Another road trip from the mid-Atlantic coast to Nebraska for Christmas was a nonstop excursion. We drove through the night. No, let me correct that, *Mom* drove through the night. I was always surprised that we would drive all day, with Mom providing the snacks substituting for meals, usually peanut butter on Ritz crackers, while sitting in the passenger seat, and yet she would still be the overnight driver. By now, we had a station wagon with a top luggage rack. With the back seat folded down, all four of us kids could recline, sort of. We were sixteen to six years old. The three oldest were in a row, with the youngest lying crosswise at our feet. I was the tallest and in the center, so I had to keep my knees bent to avoid kicking my younger sister. For some reason, I felt like my head was six inches lower than my legs, like the length of the car was angled. In my mind, all the blood was rushing to my head.

We were packed in like sardines, and we certainly weren't going to touch each other. There were cooties involved!

As the wee hours rolled in, Mom kept awake by rolling down her window, allowing freezing Midwest winter air to rush into the car while blasting the radio with Christmas carols and singing along. Someone in the car cried out, "Mom! Roll up the window!" She sure liked to drive.

She wrote of her passion for both driving and all other methods to get from one place to another. She craved independent mobility, by foot, by bicycle, by car, or by plane.

Transportation

Looking back over the years, I've discovered that my modes of transportation have been in direct relation to age and economic status. These modes of transportation have evolved from walking to the modern jet plane, with a brief period in between for the bicycle and a longer period for the automobile.

In my pre-teen years, walking was my chief form of transportation. My family owned a battered old car, but it was constantly in need of repairs, or it was too expensive to operate. So we walked. We not only walked to town, which was only a few blocks, but we walked to church, walked to school, walked to visit friends, and walked for recreation. One summer Sunday we even walked from Los Angeles to Hollywood. I classify hitch-hiking as a form of walking. It's just a more expedient method to get from one place to another without bus fare. My mother and I launched our hitchhiking career with short trips of about thirty five miles or so, culminating with a big trip of fifteen hundred miles from California to the Midwest at Christmastime.

In my early teens, shortly after my father's death, my first bicycle was acquired by trading my father's carpentry tools. It was old and rusty, out of alignment, and badly in need of paint, but I thought it was beautiful. It was a delight until a careless motorist crumpled it under the wheels of his car and was held legally responsible for buying me a new bicycle. This new bicycle served as transportation for those early dating years. The United States was well into World War II. With gas rationing and tire shortages, automobiles were scarce. We rode bicycles on dates to the swimming pool or tennis court, and for a movie date it was more romantic and exciting to sit side-saddle across the bar of a boy's bicycle and let him do all the pedaling.

By the time I had reached my late teens and cars were becoming plentiful, I developed a wild passion for driving. I begged endlessly to anyone who owned a car for a chance to drive. My first car was equal in quality to my first bike. It was old and rusty, in need of paint, and badly in need of repairs. To me, it was beautiful. This old car chugged along to church, to the movies, to school activities, and then one day it refused to chug anymore and I was back to walking.

*As I approached the last teen years, the passions
I had felt for the bicycle and the car were transferred
to the airplane. I must learn to fly. I joined the Civil Air
Patrol, took the required courses in weather and navi-
gation and even logged a few hours in the simulator.
Unfortunately, actual flying lessons were financially
beyond my reach, but that didn't stop me from using
any means to persuade someone to take me flying and
let me try my hand at the controls.*

*Now after thirty thousand miles of air travel,
I'll have to admit that I'm perfectly content to stay
on the ground and drive a late-model car, or maybe
take a bicycle ride on a shiny ten-speed racing bike.
Occasionally I feel inspired to walk, but I have been
known to move my car from one end of a shopping
center to another to avoid walking. I'm sure it's a
shameful attitude, but at times I even feel a bit smug
because now I can afford the luxury of choosing my
mode of transportation.*

What a crazy kid! A teenager without a nickel in her pocket
would join the Civil Air Patrol, thinking she's going to learn to fly
an airplane. Sometimes, when I'd see that WWII poster of Rosie
the Riveter, that young woman with her hair in a bandana and her
arm raised, flexing her bicep, I'd think of my mom. I even told her
so once, and she looked at me like I was nuts. She didn't see herself
that way, at all.

I'm not sure when this story was written, perhaps during her undergraduate work. She certainly wasn't exposing her poverty-stricken circumstances. Can't help but smile with Fannie's choice to use the paltry sum value from the carpentry tools to provide her daughter a bike.

Fannie loved to road trip on a bus. Airplanes were not an option, even in her wildest imagination. Barbara loved to fly. She always took an interest in the people she sat beside. She loved the immediacy of flying, being in a totally different climate or time zone within such a short period of time, and the feeling of privilege flying provided. But she was distressed with turbulence.

When she had to fly to Chicago to meet a mediator to finalize her second divorce, I happened to be living there and was newly reappointed to a position that allowed me a new company car. I had purchased my prior company car and it was only two years old, so I could offer it to my mother. She planned to sell her older car and compensate me with the cash from that sale.

The day of the official meeting, she drove herself downtown—having never driven in Chicago before—looking for an address she'd never been to before. It was raining, yet she felt powerful, independent, competent, and confident. She left my home within a day or two, sitting tall in the saddle in that car, headed for Maryland to visit my sister's family before she drove home to Texas. It was a new lease on life! She was sixty-two and fearless in road-tripping by herself, halfway across the country.

I'm a good driver also. I choose to be the driver when going places with friends. On the rare occasion when I've been the passenger with a man driving, I've steeled myself against liking it too much. I knew it was a rare, sweet pleasure, a feeling of femininity. While I certainly enjoyed it, I didn't want to be sad when it was no longer available.

I'm a lousy distance driver, especially when by myself. I become bored and lulled by the rhythm of the road under the tires. We're a prolific road-tripping family, so I feel lowly in confessing being a weak link. Mom used to say, "Carol's sound asleep before we back out of the driveway."

I JUST DON'T WANT TO GO

I didn't want to make the next move with my mother, step-father, and two younger siblings. My stepfather had retired from the navy, completed his master's degree, and secured a teaching position at a small state college in southwestern Minnesota. Mom would later refer to this piece of the country as "the frozen tundra"; she hated the winters, didn't like our house, and abhorred the practice of many to endure the long winters looking through the bottom of a bottle. That's a Minnesota statistic—I didn't make it up. I was almost nineteen and thought this was the time to make the break. My older sister had made her break at nineteen; she had gotten married.

The house rule to receive basic college funding for books and tuition at a state or community college was maintaining a 3.0 GPA or better and remaining a dependent of the household. There was never an option, nor the money to go away to school as some of my best friends were both allowed and encouraged to do, nor the awareness of even the slight possibility that different institutions might offer greater opportunities after graduation.

As a senior in high school, I had glamorized the thought of attending a state teacher's college in Maryland, where I would use my own savings for the room and board expenses and apply for academic scholarship funds. But I took one look at the rural setting, the cell-like dorm linoleum tile floors, cinderblock walls, and one tiny high window, and checked that off my list! No. I'd always worked full-time or part-time as soon as I was permitted and always had my own cash spending money. Mom often said she never knew anyone who got as much pleasure from spending money as I did. She said money just "burned a hole" in my pocket. But *my* money was not going to be spent on food and cinderblock walls when the offer of paid tuition was available at home.

I reached a turning point, though, that resolved my decision to accompany my family move to Minnesota. Mom and I had a discussion one morning between just the two of us, a discussion complete with wracking sobs. Mine.

My emotions tend to spill out, bubble out, seep out, and explode. Mom and I are different in this personality characteristic—must be a nature thing. Oh, I knew when she was angry, and she would be happy about the usual things like Christmas morning or a task well done, but she wasn't overflowing with outward emotional projection. Mom used to say she could always read my face. Regardless of the emotion: happy, sad, scared, sorrowful, angry, hurt, embarrassed, I wear my heart on my sleeve, my face, everywhere! I learned of this difference sometime in my thirties.

A trusted, wise professional (yes, my wellness counselor while in my thirties) enlightened me to my pattern of only acknowledging the polar opposites of emotion. I was either happy or pissed off. If my feelings were hurt, it pissed me off. If I was embarrassed or felt insecure, it pissed me off. I needed to learn the huge list of emotions, inclusive of victimhood, powerlessness, shame, contentment, joy—the list is about one hundred words long—and I needed to learn to *recognize* them correctly. I had never witnessed all those emotions in my rearing, as my mom rarely showed anything other than mad or glad. On rare occasions, I could see "hurt" in her eyes and face, a feeling of being done-wrong when her guard was down. It didn't last long, as she would quickly move to being angry at the situation, person, or thing that had brought about the pain. Although I learned well, I needed to learn differently.

So she and I were sitting at the dining table and we were the only ones in the house. My younger siblings and stepfather had left for school. Mom had a cup of coffee and was sitting in her usual spot at the end of the table. She said, "I want to talk about your coming with us to Minnesota."

I didn't drink coffee yet, but I sat down, unconsciously choosing my usual seat at the table, just to her left. I replied, "I just don't want to go," without offering any reason that either of us would hear as substantial. We bantered back and forth a bit, avoiding the elephant in the room, and then, in a heartbeat, the discussion got intense.

Mom said, "I know Dad hasn't always been the best father—" But before she even finished the sentence, I blurted out with head-jerking sobs, "But *no* father calls their daughter a bitch and tells them to get screwed!"

The waterworks were on. My sobbing was borderline hysterical. I had kept the overwhelming sorrow locked up since Thanksgiving, seven months earlier. Given that I'm a talker, that's a long time. My stepfather and I hadn't said but two or three words to each other during the whole time. Not "Where's Mom?" or hi or goodbye or "Pass the salt."

That prior November, we were having ten people for Thanksgiving dinner. This included our family of six, my sister's husband, my boyfriend (the poor guy ... looking back I feel so badly for him, having to enter into the household, wading through the tension like walking through a minefield), and a married couple, slightly younger than my parents. My stepfather had met the couple during his master's work.

God only knows *why* he invited them! Who did he think he was or who was he trying to be? They were intellectuals, scholars, in their early forties, without children. Since our dining table could only accommodate a tight-squeeze maximum of eight people, it was decided to haul all the dishes and food to the downstairs rec room and use the Ping-Pong table as a dining table. Seems like such an unfathomably crazy decision, but such was normal in middle class America in 1973. My mom used an orange and yellow floral-patterned bedsheet as the tablecloth. At least it had autumn colors. I was told to set the table with "the good dishes," which were white with gold accents and turquoise bamboo shoots. Things weren't matching very well, to say the least, but we owned "good dishes," and my mother enjoyed using them whenever an occasion presented itself. I also set out "the good glassware," inclusive of a wine glass for anyone over nineteen years of age. There would be *no* illegal taste of wine, ever, in my mother's home. The only option for a wine glass was actually a sherry glass, with a teeny tiny stem, about four inches tall, and a capacity for about one and a half ounces of liquid.

The guests arrived, and we hauled all the freshly made Thanksgiving foods from the kitchen to the basement, and then, *and then*, my stepfather made the host gesture of opening the gallon jug of wine he'd purchased and awkwardly walked around the table to pour the smidgeon amount for those of age. My boyfriend did not consume alcohol. He was not a goody-two-shoes—he was more of a been-there-done-that guy before I knew him, and he didn't like alcohol (or drugs or weed). As my stepfather reached to pour, my guy was not quick enough to decline before an ounce was in the glass.

Later that day, while clearing the table, I received the verbal wrath for my guest *wasting* the wine. Poor Bobby (the name has been changed to protect his innocence). The air in our house, *especially* when my stepfather was home and *always* when a courtship was present, was often thick, filled with particles of tension and judgment, eggshells and trepidation. I had been breathing it for so long, I didn't know.

In fairness to my stepfather, he didn't know any better. The practice of having wine was *way* above our family's pay grade, beyond our lifestyle, and beyond our income. He may have been putting on airs, trying to be something he wasn't, or trying to be something he *wanted* to be. Whatever the impetus, the end result usually did not meet his expectations, and his insecurity would take revenge on others.

His failing was the need to make others feel they were less, so he could feel better about himself. His most often used tools were ridicule; nasty criticisms; snide, snarky, sarcastic remarks; and control. Instilling a fear of physical punishment was far more common than the actual show of physical force.

But that is it. That is all I have to say about him.

From my perspective, he chose to waste the opportunity to be of value; to be of good; to teach his son, his daughter, and his stepdaughters what it meant to be a father, a husband, a role model. Had he done so, he might have made me and my siblings feel of value. He surely would have impacted our life choices differently. He was there and he brought in the paycheck, but he was not nurturing or kind. With all that he accomplished, all that he survived, inclusive of twenty years serving in the armed forces, and all the intelligence he possessed, he couldn't break his defensive-attack patterns. I never saw his power trip projected onto other men, though. No, his lack of self-confidence stymied any challenge toward another man. Unfortunately for us, women and children were his targets of choice.

So after dinner, after the guests had left, Mom and I were in the kitchen doing the dishes. My younger siblings were downstairs watching TV. I don't recall being asked to help—I wanted to do it. Helping was not a burden or a chore on this particular occasion. We were talking, just the two of us, chatting about the midday Thanksgiving meal, among other things. I remarked, "Boy, those Thompsons sure are smart," referring to the invited couple.

My mom kept her eyes on the stockpot she was handwashing and replied, in an appreciative, respectful-of-the-Thompsons tone, "Yes, they sure are."

In walked my stepfather, who muttered accusatorially at me, "What did you say?"

I furrowed my brow at his unwarranted attack and said, "Nothing."

He repeated his question more forcefully, stepping closer to me, with my back to the refrigerator. "What did you *say?*"

My mom turned her head slightly away from the sink of pots and pans and offered her dismissing reply to his irrational challenge with, "All she said was the Thompsons sure are smart people!"

Thwarted, he snarled, "Well, what's the big secret then?!"

Mom and I were both a bit dumbfounded as to how this got so out of control so quickly, and I said, "Well, what's the big deal?"

That did it. He jerked closer to me, a common practice, just to see me flinch, just so I'd know he had the power to make me flinch, and said, "Why don't you just get screwed, Bitch!"

The words hit me like an open-handed slap. I physically fell against the refrigerator door. While that language or name-calling may be commonplace in some circles, or even in some households, it was definitely not in ours. We were called "stupid" quite often, but the leap to "bitch" was a Grand Canyon leap. My tears of hurt—of course, camouflaged as anger—flowed. He went to their bedroom, and I went to mine across the hall.

Later that evening, my mother knocked on both doors, one after the other, to urge a family watching of *My Fair Lady* on network television. As I could hear his decline, he could surely hear mine. Hence the silence between us began, hence my not wanting to move to Minnesota.

Mom was intolerant of crying, and I was a crier. My feelings were hurt easily and often. But she did not scold me for crying that morning during our talk at the dining table as we both relived the incident from seven months prior. My sobs were so visceral—all she could do was look at her hands, her coffee cup, and pick at the tablecloth with her fingernail. Looking back, it's maybe odd she didn't hug me or express much tenderness to my hurt. But that wasn't her. She just didn't indulge such things.

A couple of options come to mind. One: she always said that sympathy was the last thing I needed when I felt bad, as it escalated my emotions. Two: the traumas she had suffered as a child and adolescent were so much greater than anything I was suffering that she could only muster a comparable amount of empathy. Perhaps I wanted her to feel sorrowful. I didn't begrudge her choice in my stepfather, as I'd yet to grasp his debilitations. He was the norm to me; he represented my perception of "man." She loved her husband. She was often trying to balance the peace in the household, especially when it came to my older sister and me. I know she felt badly for me, but she knew his limitations and made allowances for them. She loved him.

Now, I had unwittingly put her in the position of having to navigate this situation, of finding the peace again. While I was not privy to any discussion they'd had, and communication between me and my stepfather was not yet resolved, at least the elephant was exposed and the tension eased. Within a couple of days, she came to me and said they would buy me a vehicle (as I would need a car for both school and whatever job I secured, and juggling with their cars was becoming increasingly more difficult now that my brother had his license). They would let me live on campus (less than three miles from the home they purchased in Minnesota) *if* I would move with the family. So I did.

I was never offered an apology, and the tension wasn't gone, but the cork was out of the bottle. These two provisions would give me the prospect of some independence from his scorn and criticism. Living on campus would also give me the freedom to make my own choices, whether good or bad.

We packed up and made the drive across the county. During our first few days in Minnesota, my stepfather's boss gave us a tour of the small campus, specifically the classroom buildings. Near the end of our first look at the school, he said, "Does Carol want to see the dorms?"

My stepfather responded, "No, we don't need to see them, she's not living on campus anyway."

I knew better than to speak up, to contradict or challenge my stepfather in front of anyone, let alone his new boss. Knowing better wasn't a fear of direct punishment, but more that his revenge for embarrassing him would show up somehow, someway, indirectly later. Besides, I wasn't a mean, nasty kid, and I didn't ever *want* to cause them embarrassment. He was reneging, though. Perhaps he'd never fully agreed to the stipulation my mom had offered. My lack of a poker face must have been visible to our guide.

Can you imagine my satisfaction when, after walking just a short distance farther, our guide said, "This is "F" dorm; I thought you'd like to see it." Then we made a quick walk through the dorm.

The house they'd purchased had three bedrooms on the main level and one bedroom in the basement with an attached three-quarter bath. That private bathroom was the *luxury* that was expected to replace my desire to live on campus. Lest I seem spoiled, let me tell you the shower was nothing more than an unlit concrete stall, the commode struggled to flush, and there was a one-bulb light fixture above the nondescript sink. Since the basement was more than seventy-five percent below ground level, there was only one tiny window in the bedroom, about one foot high by two feet wide. Technically, there was no secondary egress from the room; therefore, technically it wasn't a legal bedroom.

The walls were cinderblock, and my mom painted them bright yellow in an attempt to cheer up the dankness. One morning, she came into the room at eight o'clock as I was sleeping off a three-o'clock-in-the-morning bar shift, inclusive of downing a couple of vodka gimlets (the suggested beverage as I entered the adventure of alcohol consumption). I had probably hit the sack around four o'clock. The smell of the paint was a rude wake-up call, but she was on a mission. I got out of bed and helped move furniture.

Her effort was in vain, as the basement was so damp, black mold chronically climbed up the perimeter walls from the tile floor in both the bedroom and bathroom. At the time, I was ignorant to the ills of mold. Perhaps my mom was too. Regardless, she didn't choose to tell me of the danger, but she periodically came in my room and we moved all the furniture to wash and sanitize the walls, griping all the while. I've mentioned she hated this house; the mold was one of the reasons.

I saved my money from waitressing and bartending during my sophomore year and moved on campus for the next two years, buying my own room and board. I didn't even consider sharing a small apartment, which might have been more cost-efficient, as that would have crossed the line of not being a dependent of the house-hold, and tuition payments might have been jeopardized, or at least it would have caused more discussion than I wanted. Stubbornly, I did not want to live at home. An offer, an agreement, had been proposed, and I was determined to see the promise fulfilled, even at my own expense. Both Mom and my stepfather expressed their opinions of my wasting money in this decision, but I'll bet you dollars-to-donuts Mom was glad I was out of that room. Funny how neither of my younger siblings was urged to enjoy the *luxury* of a private bath once the room was vacant.

Stubborn is a lesson my mama taught me well. Headstrong was a recurring theme in both our lives.

BABIES DON'T COST THAT MUCH

That was her response to my wanting to have a child as a single woman. Her comment was overly simplistic. I'm not sure if she was referring to the actual physician and hospital fees associated with having a baby, or if she was speaking to the daily costs of food and clothing. However, I am certain her comment was an effort to minimize my anxiety and to show support for any decision I might make. She'd raised me to believe I had the knowledge and ability to handle life on my own.

I had always wanted to be a mother—no doubt, no question. From as early as I can remember, I liked kids. My mom had often told the story of when she came home from the hospital with my younger brother when I was two and a half years old. I literally cooed at the tiny bundle in her arms, rendered speechless by the preciousness of the newborn baby. As soon as I was deemed old enough, I babysat for our next door neighbor's two little girls while the adults were at our house for the evening playing cards. My services were free (so said my mom) so I could get experience. Once I started charging for babysitting, I was so darned good at it that I was booked three to five nights every week throughout my early teen years. I had a wad of cash, earned at fifty cents per hour, in my dresser drawer that I would spread out and recount in the privacy of my bedroom. A little Silas Marner, I was.

Some babysitters, actual friends of mine, would talk on the phone all evening, or risk sneaking their boyfriend in for a visit, or put the kids to bed early just because they'd grown tired of the work of engaging with kids. Not me. I played with them the whole time. I didn't have a boyfriend anyway (until the summer of my seventeenth birthday). My mom had told me to always do the dishes, so I always did. And occasionally, if I knew the family well and they had the ingredients, I'd bake chocolate chip cookies. It was only after the kids were in bed that I wanted my shift to be over. Sitting alone in a strange house after dark was scary, and I just wanted to go home.

I'd call my mom to get her scouting report of the late-night movies available on TV. There were only four or five channels in the late 1960s through early 1970s, so choices were slim. Videos and DVDs didn't exist. But Mom knew all the old movies and could tell me, "That's a good one, you'll like that one," or "No, I don't think you'd like that, it's a mystery and might be scary." She knew them all.

She'd spent many a day and night in theaters, seeking safety from the horrors of her younger life. Movies provided her exactly what they were intended to provide: a total escape from reality. Growing up in the communities surrounding Hollywood offered her a fantasy of what could be. My mom loved movies, especially movie musicals. She loved Nelson Eddy and Jeanette MacDonald, or Fred Astaire and Ginger Rogers, Gene Kelly, even Elvis Presley, and then came Julie Andrews. Mom thought she was the best, with perfect teeth, beauty, and a voice above all others. Mom liked romantic movies, too, especially romantic comedies, but nothing was more enjoyable than the movie musicals. We all embraced her pleasure in movie watching. Today, even our next generation is guilty of watching great movies over and over again. But I still avoid scary or suspenseful plots. I don't need those thoughts in my head or the nightmares they trigger.

Freshman and sophomore years in college, I'd declared elementary education as my major. The first year, I worked five afternoons a week at a daycare center and loved every minute and every little kid. However, during my sophomore year while working in a hotel chain restaurant and lounge, *far* more than part-time, I changed my major to hospitality management. I don't equate this career choice change with my not being a parent, but it did take me away from my joy in spending time with little kids.

By the time I was thirty-five and feeling really sad about a lot of things, one of them was not being a mother. Not only was I not a mom, but I had no foreseeable opportunity on the horizon. Naturally, I talked to my mom. I intended to become a mother on my own. This decision was based mostly on a feeling of competence versus courage or confidence. My mother had raised me to "figure it out," to be self-reliant. If she had any moral or spiritual reservations about my plans, she never voiced them. I'll bet she had qualms about how she would explain my choice to others, but she didn't let her concerns rule her words. She'd cross that bridge when she got to it. "Babies don't cost that much" was supportive—advising me to not allow finances to restrict choices.

I started by investigating national adoption options; I didn't need to biologically have a baby, as I loved all kids. However, this process took me straight into a few brick walls. I investigated international adoption options and was discouraged by the time, travel, and financial requirements, not to mention the horror stories of illegalities beginning to surface. My last investigation for adoption was specific to multiracial adoption, inclusive of children with disabilities.

After attending a few meetings, I did some hard assessments. While I was confident in my inclination to be a good mother, even a single, working mother, I was not confident in my ability to lead a child through so many obstacles to navigate, which could include the following. One: I'm not the same race as my mother. Two: I'm of mixed race. Three: I'm adopted. Four: I don't have a father. Five: I'm disabled.

I had wasted a year investigating, at which point a lightbulb popped on in my head: I have the vessel; I just need the sperm. I opened the yellow pages in search of a sperm bank. This seemed simple. I'd use a large syringe-type apparatus, like the one used to baste a turkey. I made the call. How's that for negating the value of men?! I'll bet the gal on the other end of the phone is still laughing, twenty-five years later.

Once I grasped the processes, I sourced a fertility specialist, who by happenstance, was an ace in his field. A few weeks into the ordeal, I became aware of his prior guest appearance on *The Phil*

Donahue Show. This was it! I'd hit pay dirt, the mother lode of best possible circumstances.

After my initial consultations, he said, "Just because we have the science doesn't mean we're required to do the procedure. I require two sessions with a certified psychologist and their supportive feedback to move forward."

No problem, I thought. In fact, I welcomed the requirement, if only to bolster my confidence. I met with a recommended psychologist not far from my place of work in downtown Chicago. After two one-hour sessions, I remember this one specific exchange.

She asked, "What makes you think you can do this on your own?"

"Well," I said. "My mother supplied all the nurturing and structure in my childhood, and my stepfather provided the income. I can do both."

She accepted the answer with a pensive expression and then added, "One day, you might want to take a look at that." One day, in the not-too-distant future, I would, with Jane.

The psychologist sent her approval to the physician, and I simply just planned to get pregnant. It was fun selecting a sperm donor. The doctor assured me that all of the genetic concerns I had were prescreened, and all I needed to focus on was selecting a donor who would match my own genetic likenesses.

"You want a child to look like you," he said. So I selected eye color, hair color, height, weight, ancestral national origin, and a fair complexion, all to match mine. My initial expectation was for a one-time office visit and Shazam! I'd be pregnant. Not so.

They have systems to detect the exact, most opportune day

in the monthly cycle to inseminate. Unfortunately, the ovulation detection process was not without a glitch, so they advised the introduction of an ovulation enhancement drug called Clomid. The excitement and optimism with the first, second, and subsequent insemination visits were hard to contain, but it was also fun to keep the secret.

After an insemination, I felt like the cat that ate the mouse. I had a private grin, a happiness of anticipation. I also kept the secret from my employer. I'd accumulated ninety-six paid sick days in my seventeen years of employment and planned to take them all. I'd earned them. I'd only taken five sick days in my full tenure, and that included a major surgery. I paid for the actual insemination fees out-of-pocket and joked I would name this kid Visa. I recall one office visit when I stopped to pay my invoice at the receptionist's desk, and she offered such tender encouragement.

She said, "You know, we see a lot of people through here, with a variety of circumstances, and I just want to tell you, *this* is right. We're all hoping for you."

I had six inseminations within a nine-month period of time. After each one, I looked for the sign, the omen that would foretell my conception. I would know on Valentine's Day, or Mother's Day, or my birthday, but no omen proved positive. The hard part was supposed to be raising a child, not conceiving one.

I had been cautious in my habitual pattern to plan ahead. I'd looked for a new house so my commute to work would be less time-consuming and I could have live-in nanny quarters. I'd planned the décor for the baby's room. I'd selected the fabrics, anticipating the pleasure I'd take in sewing what I needed. I would purchase a used crib and repurpose existing pieces I owned. But mostly, I kept these plans private and didn't pull any triggers. I didn't want people to think I was putting the cart before the horse. I only purchased two things: a Santa bib and a soft white teddy bear. I also considered the help I'd need at the time of the baby's birth. So I asked my mom to come visit.

She said, "Oh, I'll be there, but I don't think I can be in the delivery room with you. I don't think I can watch while you're in so much pain."

She never liked being pregnant. She'd always spoken of feeling fat and bloated and miserable. She rarely spoke of the pains of childbirth, except with a nonverbal roll of her eyes and a grunt recalling our births. When she had my brother, a woman was in the bed beside hers who was crying and screaming with every contraction. It drove her nuts. Throughout my life, she'd often spoken of my low tolerance for pain. I always found that strange. How could she know whether something hurt or not? Maybe I *am* a weenie.

Tending to sickness was not her strong suit. When we were ill and needed to stay home from school, she appeared almost annoyed, like being sick was our fault. She fed me warm Jell-O after oral surgery, and we were allowed the rare treat of 7UP for an upset stomach. Perhaps the appearance of annoyance was the result of her dealing with powerlessness. She didn't have total control to make us well, so she had to be angry at the illness or injury.

In kindergarten one day, I watched a little girl go up to the teacher's desk and say she felt sick. She was sent to the nurse's office and then got to go home. Within a day or two, I did the same. The nurse said I didn't have a temperature but asked if I wanted to go home.

Well, of course, that was the point! For some reason, Mom didn't have a car at home, so I was driven in a taxi. The minute I got out of that car, she knew. Man, was she mad. I never faked sick again.

When pondering career options while I was in high school, I gave a momentary thought to nursing. She'd said, "Doctors and nurses are a different breed of cat. They've chosen to spend their time around sick people; people who don't feel good. That's a special kind of person. I don't think that's the right choice for you."

She wasn't being critical. She was just calling a spade a spade. She may have been projecting, but she was probably right.

After six insemination attempts, supported by ovulation enhancement, I was told the bell curve of probability of conception had run its course. The next option was to advance the intensity of ovulation enhancement with much greater risk of multiple fertilizations. I was just fine with the ten percent risk of multiples presented by Clomid; actually I was happy with the risk of having twins. However, pushing the risk of multiples to sixty percent or more, by choice as a single mother, seemed absurdly irresponsible. After many, many tears, for months actually, I had to move on with my life. The process was draining; month after month, flying up to the peak of anticipation with each attempt, only to be plummeted to the gutter of disappointment.

I'd fantasized the future, fantasized seeing my mother with my child, and fantasized seeing a glimpse of myself in that child smiling back at me. I even prayed about conceiving. While I've always believed in God and Christianity, I was so driven in my career that I had not found the time to create the habits of surrendering to Him. I did pray, though, and this was the longest, single-focus prayer I'd ever requested. I even prayed that I'd accept His will. But I didn't. I was mad. I was exhausted from thinking about it, and yet I couldn't stop thinking about it. I felt so lonely without the prospect of a child to love, and the anticipation of that loneliness lasting forever was heart-wrenching. And, lest I forget, those hormonal drugs can really play havoc with emotions.

I have often wondered why I was deprived of being a mother. And why a child or children were deprived of having me as a mother. I don't expect to ever know the answer. While I'd failed to get the job done, I sure as heck gave it a valiant effort. I needed to move on with my life, knowing I'd done all I knew to do. The window that opened was a new job opportunity in Denver.

I'm an optimist, if not by choice or nature, then surely by rearing. Mom never allowed us to wallow in self-pity; she never indulged whining. I quit my job after seventeen years, took the better one, moved to Denver, and thought, "Well, maybe I'll find a husband who already has kids."

Now, twenty years and two more jobs later, I'm thinking I may just find the guy who's entering his grandpa years!

ONE DAY, WE NEED TO TALK ABOUT YOUR MOTHER

These words were spoken by Jane, my counselor, at least three times in the first year of my weekly appointments. The first time, I was a bit confused because I wasn't seeking her counsel for anything related to my mother. To my thinking, my mom was the only good thing in my life. Her presence, her protection, her love were the only constants I could trust with absolute certainty. The second and third times Jane mentioned my mother, I responded, "I know." Then I segued quickly to another topic.

I wasn't sure how to broach the thirty-seven years of my life's information and sort out what specifically I needed to look at, question, talk about, and resolve with regard to my mother. Going to wellness counseling was about being unhappy with me and the status of my life. This included my job being horribly oppressive under a chronic cloud of feeling undervalued, my lack of any romantic relationship, and therefore no prospect of becoming a mother. And I could say all of that contributed to stress eating. But that's a lie. I love to eat—happy, sad, stressed, or carefree—but I was at a weight peak and that does raise the unhappy measurement.

I talked to my mom about everything. We talked two to seven times a week, and we wrote letters almost weekly. Once I began meeting with Jane, I had to reduce my communication with my mom because I couldn't trust myself to keep my mouth shut.

I did write her:

I feel I have a better handle on my dissatisfaction with my life. We know I love my job – but it has no direction. That word is key to me right now. Direction. I always felt there was a destination, even if that was an illusion. I've thought so since I can almost remember. It was a given we (us kids) go to college, it was a given that I begin a career after graduation, options didn't exist, i.e., grad school, travel for a year, etc., certainly the norm was to get a job, therefore that was the direction. Never ordered, or maybe even spoken, but nonetheless, the plan. Next, my direction was to do the best I could, to earn the most I could, to beat the odds of succeeding, to eventually provide me with the husband, family, and money that were all parts of the intangible direction I felt.

It's gone. I don't know where it went. But now I'm thirty-seven, it's supposed to be happening by now, and it's not. I don't have a direction. I'm floundering. I know I will not find what I am looking for in my job. But until I know where or what it is, I need this job. Regardless of when it happened, there are reasons why I am at this place in my life. I want to seek those reasons, and not allow the same patterns to continue, whatever they may be.

I want a direction. I want a plan. It can't be the former plan as it doesn't fit anymore. It would be so simple to quit and move down to Texas and live with you until I can find what I am seeking. But that would make me miserable. Not only would I still have the lack of direction, but also I'd lack any independence or value (even if that is only with my employees and customers).

Perhaps I knew I'd developed patterns, mirrored behaviors, and held perspectives and judgments that I derived, in great part, from my mother. That does not mean they were all bad, or wrong ... but *some* might have been ineffective. But that's logic talk, that's after-the-fact wellness talk. I was afraid of the wrongs or bads, and

I was afraid to expose them, even to myself. Given that my mom was my one true thing, I was fearful of throwing her under the bus. I was walking on thin ice here.

Steadfastly, I maintained the privacy within Jane's sunroom, but it came at a cost. Talking or writing with my mom was almost without boundary (except any experience regarding alcohol or men). Now, a new boundary was anything said at Jane's. With doubts of my strength to keep the privacy, I had to reduce the quantity of communication with my mom. I knew this was hard on her. It was hard on me too! She never showed anger at me or accused me of betrayal, but she knew I was keeping the counseling processes from her. She respectfully didn't ask about the details.

Jane offered a perfect visual. She clasped her hands together with her fingers intertwined in a tight grip and said, "This is you and your mother. We are going to have to take it here," as she spread her hands apart about eighteen inches with her palms stretched open, before continuing, "in order to come back to here." She brought her palms together, less than a fraction of an inch apart, open and relaxed, just barely touching.

The lesson again was the need to push the pendulum the opposite direction with equal force for it to eventually come back to a restful, healthy center. I needed to find *value*, separate of my value to her. Distancing my heart—even for a short time—and questioning those feelings within the confines of Jane's sunroom allowed me to gain perspective. Mom might have feared I was keeping secrets that were specific or critical of her. I feared the same! But such was not the case. She did her very best for me, for all of her kids, all of the time. If and when her mothering fell short of optimum, it was never with intent to hurt or damage. It just was. Her life behaviors were influenced by *her* experiences and *her* mother's teachings, and her patterns formed.

Therefore, my intent during these most painful counseling sessions was to get it out, go fast, learn, evaluate, acknowledge, accept, and be at peace. Without our frequent communication, our palms were eighteen inches apart, and I wanted to get to that place where our palms could meet.

Mom visited me once or twice during these couple of years, and I surely visited her three or four times. Ever since leaving home, I had developed a habit of being irritable on the last day of visits. It was a coping mechanism. If I was angry, there was no room in my heart to feel distraught at the end of a visit. She knew this, so she secretly wrote me a letter a day or two before the visit ended. When she visited me, she even used my stationery! With this kindness, I'd have a letter from her in my mailbox a day after I got home (or after she'd left my home), to ease my feelings of loneliness. Isn't that nice? Her concern for me during these couple of years was heavy on her heart. My silence pained her, and she deserved some explanation. I wrote her a letter. By this time, I dated my letters. I also knew she saved all letters, so I wrote a specific instruction: "Do not save this letter, please." She did. I found it separately stored in her cardboard box with all of my other letters. Across the envelope, she had written "Private." I had to chuckle.

June 7, 1993

Dearest Mom,

... I can't tell you all the things that are bothering me, mainly because I don't know them. You are certainly right about a good number. I am just so very relieved that you know you are not one of them.

Yes, I am worried about wanting/having a baby. Will I be able to provide all that a child needs, including time. Sometimes I still think I can wait ... then I am brought back to reality that I can't. I can't believe this life is going by so fast!

I hate that I am in a chronic fear of insecurity in my job. Also a feeling of such low value. But I would be a fool to leave – only increasing my worries without the consistency of a paycheck and adequate medical benefits. I can't see putting that in jeopardy.

I hate the repeating failure I have in dieting. I am embarrassed about the way I look. I am crushed when thinking of the perception people have of me because of my appearance. I am only worried about my high school reunion with respect to how I can present myself. The options seem limited: an overweight old maid or faking it, like I'm happy. I'm going to try to fake it. But that certainly feels pressured.

There are so many "I"s in this letter I am going to get sick! I know this is self-serving crap, but this stuff is really hurting me. I can't talk about it without getting very upset, this writing is very difficult. But I think you want an explanation for my change in behavior and I am not hiding one from you. ... I just can't explain the whole of it.

You see ... then I have this wonderful mother. Who thinks I'm pretty (no one else does), who thinks I'm funny (no one else does, sure I can be comical if I work at it, but I'm not naturally witty), who thinks I'm smart and competent (few others do). I'm not fishing; I KNOW how you think about me. But as we've agreed before, I can't continue to rely on you for feelings of self-worth. Perhaps my stoic projection is the way I was trying to tell you all of this without really telling you. I know that I can tell you anything and that is a struggle too, because I want to tell you about every perspective Jane helps to provide. But I don't think it's the right thing to do. If I want to develop a level of self-esteem, it's defeating to rely on you for opinion and/or approval. Do you understand?

You are the best mother I could have hoped for. I wouldn't trade a thing about you. This whole problem is about me. I am still uncomfortable with the self-centered aspect of this, but I know I want to change my life and that is going to require changing me. I want to keep those "me" things at Jane's until I am better able to talk about them without emotional instability. Do you understand?

I also want to be able to enjoy my love for you and yours for me without feeling so fearful of the need I have for it. I want to be happy in it – not sad by the volume of it. I can't explain it. But can't I feel joyous when I'm sharing this love rather than teary and afraid of losing it? ...

I love you with all my heart, Carol

I find it interesting that I can read this letter today and not become overwhelmed with the emotion I felt at the time. Of course, if I read it aloud, all bets are off. Mom didn't indulge self-pity or even a glint of self-centeredness. I clearly felt counseling was grazing at the edge of self-centeredness, and that was difficult to accept. However, the privacy and focus of those sessions provided shelter from those feelings.

Jane had warned me that one of the side effects of counseling is: "You start to see your own patterns or coping mechanisms in others." Ain't it the truth! The risk of amateur, armchair psychology is a certainty. However, there's also strength found in being aware, if only as an amateur, of others' coping mechanisms. Certainly, I became more aware of my mother's humanity. Mom not being perfect did not mean she was reprehensively, unforgivably flawed, but my need to *think* her perfect was flawed.

I think Mom struggled with the continuum from self-deprecation to confident to her often-used word "smug." She was on guard to avoid anyone acting snobby toward her and never wanted to appear guilty of the same. Although I don't recall us talking about this, I had a similar issue and had talked with Jane about it. I saw a linear line with regard to feeling confident. On one side of the line was a vast length called insecure and on the other side, a vast length called arrogant. A pinpoint, a tiny spot in the center of the line, was called confident, and it seemed impossible to land on that spot. It seemed like whenever I felt proud of myself for some reason or another, something or someone came along to knock me down a peg. It's just easier, less hurtful to rest in the vast space of self-deprecation.

Jane asked, "Why don't you try to see the center as just as vast an area as the opposite ends?" The concept is a good visual, but I still struggle. One of those subliminal, unspoken lessons taught from my mom, I guess.

My mother was annoyed by my crying; therefore, I thought I was wrong and she was right. She was not a crier, and all my siblings are much more like her than I am. My expressions of happiness and excitement also peak higher and more openly than hers ever did.

Picture a seven-year-old, with messed-up childhood teeth and a smiley, enthusiastic gift-of-gab, sitting at the family dinner table. I'd be telling some story from the day's activity, and my stepfather could see nothing but my ugliness. He would mock me, biting his upper teeth over his lower lip in an exaggerated overbite, and say, "Mmm, mmm, mmm ... do you want to look like a retard your whole life?!"

Man, did that take the wind out of my sails in telling a funny story! I would melt into tears streaming down my face, with those hiccup-like gasps for breath. Mom would direct me to leave the dinner table and go wash my face. She was running interference the only way she knew. Her own mother had run interference by physically removing her from the potential harm inflicted by Charlie. This was the lesson she was taught from Fannie. Just run interference, without exacerbating the moment. Had she challenged such ridicule ... well, I don't know what would have happened because she never did, at least not in front of us kids. I would have reacted differently had I been in the same situation as my mom.

I've known many men (and couples) with children. When I assess a wrong placed upon a child, there's no stopping my voiced opinion. Often, I choose to qualify my input with the obvious disclaimer, "While I don't have children myself ...," and I also choose to employ my "reasonably smart" to try to avoid offense. Nonetheless, I can't stay mute, even at the risk of stepping on toes. I just can't.

Mom's and my hurts and harms were different in our childhoods. Now, as an adult, I would argue hers were leaps and bounds greater than mine. However, I could also argue, as a kid, I was more fragile than she was.

In the seventh grade, I came home from school one day, walked through the front door, and she immediately began yelling at me. My report card had been mailed to the house, and I'd scored a D grade in US history. She was standing in the kitchen while I looked up the half flight of stairs in our split-foyer home. I had the *audacity* to reply, "You don't know how hard it is."

She lit me up like a Christmas tree! I was referring to having spent three years out of the country for third through sixth grades and then coming back to the US, having no inkling of our country's history. Social studies in New Zealand were specific to pruning trees and shearing sheep. I'd been singing "God Save the Queen" five days a week for three years, for crying out loud. I couldn't articulate why I wasn't grasping US history; I just knew it was difficult for me. The wrath I received cured me of ever comparing hardships, although I wasn't yet even aware of her childhood traumas. This adult perception isn't to let her off the hook; she certainly could have handled such situations differently. Good or bad, it was her way to teach, "No whining, get it done, and get it done right."

Jane helped me learn there's nothing wrong with being a crier. Crying is good for me; it reaffirms my tenderhearted self; it allows me to purge sorrow. No longer suppressing the urge to cry, I dropped a few tears on the keyboard just moments ago. The trick is to let crying be a choice, when I cry and why I cry being within my control. Sometimes an isolated, specific reason to cry can trigger old hurts or losses that exaggerate the emotion. The difference now is that I might see those triggers coming, at least some of the time.

Jane also educated me regarding sadness and depression by clarifying, "No, you're not depressed. Depression is an illness and you don't have it. You're just very sad." I liked her clear definition. Being sad does not automatically mean one is suffering from depression. I haven't used the word *depression* in place of the word *sadness* since.

When the time came to do so, discontinuing "wellness counseling" did not mean I was well, but it certainly meant I was better. I'm still not married, I still don't have kids, but Jane was correct in that I no longer view those circumstances as an indication that something must be wrong with me. I can still feel disappointment about it, but it doesn't send me to the crying wall.

I cry when I want to. When in the presence of others, if I tear up a little, so be it. Those moments sometimes alert me to a need to purge. If I'm feeling the blues building, I may watch a movie—one that I know will trigger release. Then I can purge in the privacy of my home.

I've worked for three different employers in the past twenty years, and while I still work hard and long and feel an unwavering responsibility to those I supervise, work is my job—not who I am. There wasn't a specific moment in time when my perceptions changed, as the awareness of our learned values and patterns is a never-ending process. Thank goodness.

And I evolved over time to love my mother with fewer fears of loss and more joys in the moments. Thank you, Jane. You'll never know how much I appreciated your presence at that time in my life.

I'M GOING TO LIVE A LONG TIME

A number of times, when having a conversation about the future, Mom's future, she told me, "Oh, you don't have to worry about that ... I'm going to live a long time. You forget ... I come from healthy stock. I plan on living well into my nineties." Her comment was in response to one of my often repeated concerns of never wanting to be without her.

For family gatherings, we'd sort of become a "couple"—my three married siblings and Mom and me. There's a slim possibility this perception is individually mine. Not living geographically close to Mom, I would only have a clear vision of the family dynamic when I was visiting. That perception never bothered me, though, as I thoroughly enjoyed doing-for my mom.

But as her age-related dementia became more and more noticeable, I did have sorrowful feelings of loneliness within the couplehood of our relationship. Sometimes my sorrow would show itself in hurtful or unflattering behavior toward my mother; I feel ashamed. Sometimes I heard myself scolding her when she forgot this or that. Sometimes I grew impatient with her when she repeated something multiple times. I was so darned angry at the signs of dementia, and my wrath spilled over onto her. If I heard anyone outside the family even mentioning these lapses, it cut me to the quick. I had to restrain myself from lashing out. Defensive thoughts were racing through my mind. *Do you know who she is? Do you know what she has survived, what she has accomplished? That's my MOM you're talking about!* The role reversal of parent-child was prevalent in my protective instincts.

She and I would argue about the dumbest things—I thought she was constantly challenging me. For the prior twenty years, she'd relied on my opinion, memory, or judgment, so these challenges were hurtful. What's so darned funny is she felt the exact same toward me, perhaps in her mind referencing the twenty years before that when I relied heavily on her advice. We were two peas in a pod, two stubborn peas. During the dozens of drives back to her house after spending the day visiting my siblings, our make-up laughter salved most wounds.

Our connection was the deepest relationship of my life; all my friends were aware of it and some expressed envy. The shift began when I was in my early fifties and she was nearing eighty. Phone conversations changed. Regardless of the catalyst for my calling her, she tended to monologue about her to-do list for the day, week, or month. It wasn't unusual to hear the same list repeated in multiple phone calls. Her list of chores, activities, Mary Kay work, financial strife, or the balancing of some bank account would monopolize most attempts at two-party conversation. Then she'd say, "So, what do you have going on today?"

Sometimes, I would begin to relay some current event, challenge, or activity, as I'd done in conversation with her for over thirty years of adult life. Unfortunately, within just an exchange or two, I could tell she wasn't grasping the content. Either she didn't remember something we'd spoken of a day or two prior, or she just didn't understand the concept. At times, she'd ask the question and then before I could reply, she'd say, "Well, I have to go, or I'll be late for (thus and such)."

I tried to tell myself, and I told her, "The first twenty-five years you *had* to listen to my stuff—you were the mother and I was the kid. The second twenty-five years was a gift—pure unselfish indulgence of my needs. I guess for the next twenty-five years, I can return the favor."

She'd chuckle or scoff a little, having no idea of the change that was occurring. I was trying to figure out how to process this change. I was trying to stay "in my head" about it, approach it intellectually. I was trying to figure out how I could fix it. And I was trying to figure out how I could be without my mom.

I guess it's possible to feel differently, especially if one has children and/or a husband—I don't know for sure, though. As independent and competent as I am, my inner-self fear was that much of my value on earth was through the love from my mom. I'd chosen to no longer derive my personal value from my outer-self career, even though I'd carried responsibilities of significance. I'd supervised thirty-five-plus million dollars in annual revenues, a thousand staff members, and sixty salaried managers, at the peak. I'd opened and eventually closed a sole-proprietor business, shouldering the financial, operational, and weighty responsibilities solo. I've traveled the United States prolifically, setting up a team and staff to open over twenty-five restaurants. I've navigated six major geographic household moves and have purchased three residential properties. I've also participated in volunteerism when time, travel, and opportunities allow. Those professional and personal accomplishments attested to competence and independence, and I *had* perceived them as pillars supporting my value for a good long time.

With experience of how quickly I could be stripped of that outer-self value, work accomplishments seemed hollow compared to my feeling of value from my mom. Regardless of intellectually grasping personal value, emotionally those patterns die hard. I never felt so discouraged or lacking in value to spark any thoughts of offing myself, but on occasion, I wondered how many days might pass before anyone would know I was gone.

Sometimes I even thought my mom's age-related dementia was God's way to help me deal with the inevitability of losing her. With the onset, I could be weaned. Strange how that word comes to mind: weaned, like an eight-week-old puppy. Of course, I was wrong on all assessments. God is merciful. My mother was intelligent, competent, strong, and independent. Her time of suffering both mind and body deterioration was considered short by many measures, although anything longer than a day was too long for my liking! How selfish of me to think God's intent would be to protect or prepare me while inflicting any hardship on my mom! Like I said, I was still trying to figure it out—at the time, I didn't know I only had about five years.

June's father died when she was thirteen. She never spoke about his death with any more detail than those few words. She shared no story of finding him, seeing him, or any specifics regarding his death. Given the evil and difficulties he caused, and given my mother's lack of any kind words spoken of him, I can assume his death was a burden lifted, a stress removed, a freedom granted for both her and her mother.

My grandmother passed away on July 31, 1967. She was twenty days shy of her eightieth birthday. Our family was living in suburban Washington, DC, on the Virginia side. I recall a phone call to my mother. The use of the telephone was so different than it is today. We had two extensions, with cords, I might add. One was in the kitchen and one was in the basement rec room. No one in the house was on the phone much, and if we received a phone call, we were allotted a maximum ten minutes of talking time. Remember: call-waiting, answering machines, and voice messaging were still years away. As my mother listened on the basement extension, I saw her facial expression grow blank and her eyes stare off into nothingness. That was it.

Mom left us for a short period of time, maybe a week, but certainly not two. She went by herself on a flight to California to take care of whatever needed to be taken care of. By herself. Her aloneness wasn't as much a choice as a financial constraint. However, be it choice or constraint, her personal strength was the allowance. A weaker woman or stronger husband would have found a way to accommodate her not having to be alone.

She told me she found a couple of wrapped Christmas gifts in the nursing home dresser drawer for Fannie's son, my mother's brother. He lived within an hour's drive and yet didn't even come to visit his mother. My mother struggled with any forgiveness for such cruelty. When she came home, all was back to our normal. "Bunch of selfish brats," as my mom *might* have said, but she didn't. We knew nothing about death or loss, and she wasn't sharing information.

After my mom passed, my sister and I remarked on our obliviousness to our mom's needs at the time of her mother's passing; neither of us had even thought to say, "I'm sorry about your mother." We were twelve and fifteen and had not experienced one tiny event of loss in our lives. Besides, the hard shell surrounding her didn't let us in either. She didn't expose her sorrow openly. Many years later, she spoke more freely about her mom and her wishes to have asked more, talked more, and done more for her mother.

Mom chose to spend Fannie's residual financial worth at the time of her death to purchase a piano for our family. As years passed, all of us kids were provided music lessons of some sort. And, as more years passed, my siblings provided the same to their children, and all owned pianos of their own. Mom wanted me to have her piano, and I wanted it. However, with my mom's permission, I decided my newly wedded niece and I could share possession of the piano. I lived three states away, and my niece lived within a few miles of my mother.

Mom was anxious that my niece would not understand or appreciate the intangible value of the piano. She asked me (on repetitive occasions as her short-term memory was failing her) to communicate the boundaries of possession to my niece. I'm not sure why my mom couldn't or didn't communicate these thoughts herself. I mean, *she* was the writer in the family. It may be that she just didn't want to synopsize all the emotion and history within her purchase and protection of the piano. Or perhaps she struggled in organizing her thoughts without having to admit it. I did write to my niece, on my mother's and my own behalf, and include excerpts of that dated letter (I date all my letters now):

May 31, 2011

Dear Elise,

... In 1967, we moved back to the U.S., specifically, Virginia. That same year, Grand'Mere's mother died. So she went out to California, by herself to organize and attend the funeral and finalize all of her mother's loose ends.

... Fannie Schmidt (Grand'Mere's mother) did not come from any wealth. You may have heard a good number of the stories surrounding her life, but I'll pass on a few in this letter....

... What she does know is that her mother protected her from what could have been much worse. And somehow instilled a drive to get educated, save money, and live a better life. By all her history, Grand'Mere could have been smokin', drinkin', toothless, trailer-trash.

... Grand'Mere recalls Fannie's final bank account sum to be at $600. With that minimal inheritance, she bought the piano; the piano on which your aunts, your dad & I continued to practice. You do not come from a wealthy lineage. But the history of the meager lineage is more than valuable. I wanted to have that piano because of its family history.

However, there would come a day, maybe 20 years from now, when I would have to decide what to do with the piano. Obviously, I would choose to pass it on to our next generation. It's not just a piano ... it's an inheritance! I would never sell it, nor give it to a stranger. I would never want it sold, nor given away.

So, you expressed a desire to have a piano. Grand'Mere likes to think she is giving it to me, and you are going to "hold" it for me. While I want it, the logistics are just crazy and then in later years, you'd end up not needing a piano. Therefore, we want you to have it – share it with me. It's your choice.... Grand'Mere wanted me to write you, and make sure I explained the history and sentimentality.

It would be a nice addition to your new home, don't you think? We just want you to understand the heartfelt value of the piano.

Mom was always preparing for the next thing, always wanting the next adventure, the next opportunity to try something new, to learn something new. She always wanted more. Not selfishly or greedily, but like a sponge, she wanted to soak up as much as she could. She always wanted to be included, and most times she darn-well expected to be included in family or friend activities. Her wants were both experiences and reasonable possessions.

When I asked her, "Are you ever going to stop wanting more, will you ever be satisfied?" she responded, "No, never! Why should I be?" with defensive argument. While she managed her financial resources responsibly, staying within her self-imposed budget, she adamantly fought against any feeling of deprivation. She'd had enough of that growing up.

At first, in my early adult earning-power years, I felt a compulsion to gift her as extravagantly as possible. Her appreciation of my efforts was gratifying. Of course, I overspent on everything, building credit card debt with gifts and personal possessions I really couldn't afford. Living in wealthy, north-suburban Chicago, I felt like a have-not in a have world and chose denying my spending limitations to fight against the feeling. As years passed, I mistook my mom's continual wants as my responsibility to fulfill. I was angry that she'd never received gifts and kindnesses from her husband and felt she was long overdue for such. Also, at the time, I struggled with how to top the gifts from the prior occasion or holiday.

A cycle was developing. I would gift; she would be joyously, lovingly grateful; I would feel valued and appreciated; and then I'd seek more. I'd forgotten: she'd valued and appreciated that ugly six-year-old kid, with a mouth full of scary, jack-o'-lantern-type teeth. Once I figured that out, my gifting pattern didn't change, but my joy in gifting was without burden.

I wasn't doing-for her for any validation in return—just the pleasure. Besides, I didn't have kids to support or spoil, so I had the luxury of spending on my mom. That next Christmas was probably my favorite regarding gifts for her: new luggage and an airplane ticket to visit her junior high friend Idean in upstate New York, a long-distance phone card to call a few friends around the country, and four gift cards to local restaurants so she could take friends to lunch or dinner, and, of course, new clothes to dress for these occasions.

Sometimes I chose to gift things privately versus a public holiday or family occasion. I liked that look she'd give me. The look that conveyed: "I know what you're doing, and I love your generous heart." I didn't need the words—I just loved the look.

Sometimes I'd use my restaurant dining benefits for our family gatherings, and on occasion the tab exceeded my benefit. No matter. I'd get that look that relayed her appreciation. I have a photo of her sitting at a restaurant table during one of these events. She's wearing a dark turquoise blazer I'd gifted her, and that look is on her face. The woman loved turquoise! We even had a turquoise car in 1959. Every nice dress she sewed for us as little girls was turquoise.

Sometimes I gifted a household item or clothes for a specific occasion when I knew she wanted to look her very best and have the self-confidence that comes when you're assured in your appearance, and once again, I'd get that look. She spoke of pangs of guilt on occasion for having not been able to do more for her mother. Then, with appreciation, she'd add, "You never have to have that feeling of guilt."

Another photo captures a moment in time shortly after the emotional pain and strife of her second divorce, when I distinctly witnessed that she'd gotten her mojo back—her self-esteem. Oh, she'd lost a few pounds, and I know from personal experience *that* certainly tips the scales in more ways than one! My mother dressed carefully every day. She wore pantyhose, heels, and skirts or dresses in compliance with the Mary Kay company edict. Fixing her hair and makeup were faultless morning routines. I especially adore this photo of her standing in her kitchen with one of my nephews. She was fifty-eight years old. She was "all that and a bag of chips!" Oh yeah, and her blouse was turquoise!

I know I did a lot for my mother throughout my adult years. She rarely expected others to do-for her, but some project was always on the horizon. While in her seventies, she relied on my judgment or perspective and sought my guidance to get it done. While we talked on the phone, a project was always gnawing at her. She would say, "Next time you visit, I want you to help me _____." Fill in the blank: organize my closet, organize the garage, redecorate a room, resolve a storage issue, wrap her Christmas gifts, or create a photo scrapbook. There was always something. These projects were a collaboration during those years and the decades prior. But when in her eighties, her input to the tasks waned as cognition issues increased.

She once told me, "You could start a business helping seniors redecorate and reorganize their homes, especially when they downsize. Seniors can't hang drapery, or shop, or move as fast as you do. I'm not kidding, you really could!"

I *really* didn't want that business (and still don't). I'm certain I wouldn't enjoy sorting through a stranger's keepsakes, but I worked like a dog when visiting my mom to make "it" (whatever "it" was) the way she wanted it.

If I was struggling to discern how to approach or resolve a specific issue for her, for example, how to build and fabricate an arched-top, hard window cornice into a starburst of fabric, she'd marvel at my tenacity and ask, "How did you figure that out?!" *This* was the comment from the woman who had figured out *everything* for my entire life. This comment, from the woman whose mother figured out how to make a Christmas tree from useless scrap branches and a quilted hope chest from a discarded, old trunk from a charity store. Necessity is the mother of invention, and I had that mother!

I looked at her with a quizzical expression and replied, "Look who I came from!"

Then, there was the contradiction of her saying to one of my siblings, "I wish she would just come visit and relax. She always works so hard when she's here." You see, in casual conversation, if she'd said, "I want to (blank)," I was all ears, ready to get it done.

This pattern evolved over time. As a younger adult, I'd often crash into a coma of naps and movie-watching when I visited. I was building my career and took vacation at her house to feel removed from responsibility. As those proverbial parent-child roles shifted, I no longer felt like a child coming home to rest.

I was with her for the most painful, last days of her life. I hope my presence offered her comfort. I tried my best not to cry in those sporadic moments of her lucidity, but I know my face and swollen red eyes betrayed me. In one instance, I was sitting on the edge of the hospital bed positioned in her living room, while she was in and out of awareness. She opened her eyes, fully wide, and turned her head toward me. Her small, pretty blue eyes were a bit milky, but I know she saw me and I saw her. She said, "There you are!"

Her facial expression and the inflection in her voice were as if she'd been looking for me in some public place, and I'd just come from around a corner, and we'd found each other. Yet, I'd been within ten feet of the bed for the past four days. I was wearing a bright, grass-green shirt, so given that her eyesight was weakening, perhaps the color caught her attention.

I replied, "I'm right here, Mom," with an attempt to match the lighthearted, enthusiastic tone of her comment. Given the gravity of the moment, I also wanted to sound as reassuringly gentle as my loud, strong voice could.

Did she see me as the fifty-seven-year-old woman I was, or did she see fifty-seven years of me? I saw and heard in those three words, fifty-seven years of my mom, with intent to sear all those years into my memory. I'm so glad the moment occurred; I'm so glad she knew I was there, even if just in that moment.

That next night, whispering, I reminded her she would be able to see her mother and a few friends who had passed recently. Without forethought, I stroked her thin hair at her temple, smoothing it beside her ear. Instantly, I recalled her doing the same for me, some forty-five years prior, when I'd laid my head in her lap while she talked on the phone. I hope it felt as good to her as it had to me. She'd always shivered at a light touch; she liked a definitive, forceful touch whenever I styled her hair, so I was intent to apply the correct amount of pressure in my touch. Even though I didn't know if she could hear me, I told her I loved her, I'd miss her, and I asked her to be there waiting for me. Her faith was strong; I'm counting on it. Within twenty minutes, she passed away, November 3, 2012.

My intent is to be like Fannie. She made her own plan, disposing of any possessions, and securing her care in a residential facility. She'd spent a lifetime, *her* lifetime, depending only on herself. She did so even in her death. I hope to plan ahead, to make my own arrangements. If I'm alone, so be it, but I don't want to be lonely. I know my mom wasn't alone; I made sure of that. And she'd often profess she wasn't lonely. I hope Fannie wasn't alone or lonely either.

THERE'S ALWAYS A PLAN

Without a day planner or a family calendar, and certainly without a tech device, Mom always had a plan. I don't recall ever seeing a grocery list or a time sheet of which activity for which kid required her transport or presence, yet I don't recall ever missing an appointment or lesson or even being late. Mom saw things through to completion. Good enough was rarely good enough. "Do it right or don't do it at all." I make lists, I draw plans for DIY projects, and like my siblings, I pretty much always have a plan. Sometimes we have to make alterations, but we all have embraced her disposition and orderliness with intent to be prepared and organized.

There was discussion, between us kids, of our mom's wishes for burial. She'd occasionally expressed a bit of sorrow that her mother's burial vault was halfway across the country. No one ever visited it. While Mom had lived in one place for her last thirty-five years, only one of us lived in the same state. We made the decision for cremation.

Then we pondered other thoughts. Do we choose to spread her ashes somewhere or choose to place her ashes somewhere? Do we purchase an outdoor park bench, perhaps to be placed on the grounds of her church? But she was not tied to any *place,* and her church already had plans to build and relocate. We each chose to keep a portion of her remains and make choices that felt right to each of us in the coming months or years. My older sister's choice was to place her portion of Mom's ashes in the vault containing Fannie's casket and add Mom's name to the inscription stone. She spoke of wanting something to commemorate that "She was here, a life was lived." I understand her feeling.

I was uneasy with relinquishing my quarter of my mom's remains. I have no place called home in my own life, except where I live at the time. We'd moved so many times as kids, and I'd moved an additional ten times as an adult. Home is where I hang my hat, home is where my heart is, and Mom is such a huge part of my heart. I keep her ashes in my nightstand, along with a small collection of her costume jewelry. I plan to cure a concrete mold, incorporating her ashes and jewelry, so I may take it wherever I go, wherever I live. I had gifted her a resin molded angel for Christmas a few years ago, exactly like the one I have in mind to make.

Back when I was thirty, she needed major surgery. I flew her to my home and cut through the red tape necessary to secure her procedure in a military hospital near me. Then she could recuperate at my home for six weeks. Thus began a repetitive scenario. Whenever either of us had surgery, the other was present to offer the nursing. Of course, my siblings contributed time and care to both of our needs, but Mom called me her Guardian Angel, and every Christmas we gifted each other some token reminder of that role in each other's life.

Perhaps I'll change my will to include my ashes being placed in the same vault as Fannie's and Barbara's. Without my sister's decision and follow-through, this option would not have dawned on me. I am grateful.

A couple of days after my mother died, I was in her home office packing up her Mary Kay inventory to return to the company. My older sister was with me, sorting through a variety of things in Mom's desk. She came across a small card, and offhandedly said, "Oh, this is for you."

I took the card from her hand. It was slightly larger than a credit card and made of glossy cardstock, like that of a playing card. On the front was a colorful photograph of flowers, and my name was printed boldly at the top. It was one of those cards you can pick up at a souvenir gift shop kiosk. Usually there are a variety of trinkets—keychains, notepads, or shot glasses—with an alphabetized variety of first names. This card reflected my name and below the name was the descriptive word "Strong." Beneath that was a Bible verse: Joshua 1:9.

Oddly, this was the only card of this type in her desk drawer. There wasn't one for each of us kids, just this one, for me. I don't know how long she'd had it or when she was planning to give it to me. She may have been *planning* nothing, or she may have planned the whole thing. She knew I was concerned about being without her, but she always professed her intent to live a long time.

The verse reads, "Have I not commanded you? Be strong and of good courage; Do not be afraid, nor be dismayed, for the Lord your God is with you wherever you go."

I am not one to quote biblical scripture; I only know a couple-few verses by heart anyway. She knew I was strong, but she also knew all of my inner-self weaknesses. While I know the words are directly quoted as God's words to Joshua, as I read the first line, I can hear my mother's voice almost scolding me. Like when I'd play in the house with some outside toy and she would warn, "Take that outside," adding, "You're going to break something." When her prediction came true, she would scold, "Didn't I tell you!?"

Sounds like, "Have I not commanded you?" to me. The timing was perfect! I don't think she would have purchased the card had the verse been woeful or sappy or longing. Nope, that wasn't her. She chose to scold me into not wallowing in sadness. You've got to love it!

I read her prayer journals, as we came across them in her bedroom nightstand. Some may say reading was an invasion of her privacy. But I knew my mother. "Once it's written ..." was just as evident in her prayer journals. She only wrote general comments, very few specifics or incidents. She mentioned all of our names and those of her friends within her written prayers, but the details had only been spoken privately to God or in her thoughts as she logged in the journals. Up until the end, she chronically prayed for strength to control her eating habits. Good Lord, I pray history doesn't repeat, with my doing the same at age eighty-five! And to my guilty conscience, she often prayed for me to quit smoking.

The only other specific entry relative to me was a prayer for

my siblings to understand and support my aloneness once she was
gone. She knew. While she had never acknowledged my fears face
to face, she knew.

With regard to her faith, she'd said, "I don't think you know
how important my faith is to me." She was correct; I didn't. We
were taught to say grace, and we were taught to say, "Now I lay me
down to sleep," but the practice ended probably by the time my
youngest sister was in elementary school. Her faith was private,
shared only in rare moments. She urged our adult participation in
Christian worship but never hounded us. Each of us found our own
path, in our own time, all others much quicker than me.

Faith saw her through many challenges, evidenced when she
also said, "If it weren't for the Salvation Army, I'd be dead." Because
of her comment, soldiers for the Salvation Army always enjoyed
Sunday brunch free of charge in my restaurants. They didn't come
as often as I would have liked, perhaps the gift made them not want
to appear greedy. The S.A. historically holds the highest standards
of funding management. Ninety percent of all resources are granted
to their philanthropic work, only ten percent for administrative
costs. Don't believe me? Look it up; I know I'm right.

Seven months before her passing, I began attending a church in
my community. Immediately, I was embraced, literally, by a woman
in my seating area as uncontrollable tears rolled down my cheeks.
She expressed empathy in her assumption that my sorrow related
to my singlehood. I didn't correct her, as I didn't have the words.
Perhaps I still don't. I cried for the want of feeling held by the Lord
(perhaps He sent her). I cried for the inevitable, impending loss
of my mother. I told Mom that I'd found a church to attend, but

since she'd forget, I'd need to tell her again and again. I knew it was important to her.

I was not baptized as a young child. Again, she apologized and reminded me, "It just wasn't a good time." I chose immersion baptism two months after she passed. The night before the Sunday service, all of the participants, from kids to grandpas, met in the huge atrium. We sat at round tables of ten people to share our story and our catalyst for baptism now. Most had family or close friends with them. I did not. While I'm comfortable holding court in a professional setting, my discomfort in being the center of attention personally was a fear that had delayed this decision. Now it was a hurdle I had to jump. Speaking to this small group was important to me, and I was determined to "keep it together." The tears pooled in my lower eyelids as I spoke of my mom, but I didn't blink them out and risk opening the floodgates.

The next day, I steeled myself against awareness of the couple thousand people in the worship center. My focus was unwavering on the pastor before me. I chose to leave no stone unturned. My heart is on the Lord, and my soul will be with Mom's in the life to come. Just as hers is with Fannie.

Close to seven years into this composition, another resolution crept slowly and silently into my thoughts. At the time, I printed a hard copy and secured the pages in a binder. During the next couple of days, I enjoyed seeing it, holding it, feeling the weight of it, much greater than the poundage of the paper. As a book, I could physically hold some of my mother's precious writings, her stories, her memories and mine. They will be here for our family, for our generations to come, for those who loved Barbara June, and for readers who've never met my mom but can relate to these stories with memories of their own mother.

I realized while holding the bound pages that it serves another purpose. She was here, a life was lived—a remarkable life. She left a heck of a ripple in her wake. A mother's teachings have staying power. "All that I am or ever hope to be, I owe to my angel mother," so said Abraham Lincoln. I had framed that quote both for my mother and for myself one Mother's Day. My mother once told me ... in letters, by glance, in discipline, in guidance, by protection, in constancy, by deed, by look, and yes, even in words, again and again ... that she loved me. And turnabout is fair play. "And, I'm not kiddin.'"

ACKNOWLEDGMENTS

MOST FORMIDABLY, I thank my mom. The innumerous reasons for acknowledgment toward her become abundantly clear throughout the book. In my early twenties, I had a conversation with a co-worker perhaps ten years my senior and a mother of three children herself. After expressing a comment of annoyance with my mother still treating me as a child, she said, "Just remember, no one ever loves you like your mother does." I was too early in adulthood to fully appreciate her comment, but I never forgot it. It wasn't a scolding, but more a warning to heed the advice, the words from my mother, as they are irreplaceable and come from a place of unconditional love.

The mother-daughter relationship is most powerful. For most daughters, there is no greater bond, no greater connection, than that of mother and daughter. With risk of being trite, I refer to a recent quote: "When feeling unworthy or unloved, I remember whose daughter I am and straighten my crown."

Next, my siblings. I recall as a bartender in my college years one of my co-workers having one child. She was speaking to a guest sitting at our bar, relaying the decision she and her husband had made to only have one child. The guest, a man in his sixties, replied, "I'm an only child and I never had a negative thought about it, until after my parents died. Then I realized I have no one to share my memories; no one to say, "Remember the time when ... with ..." My siblings are the only people on earth with whom I share my whole life. And I share their lives.

Given that this book is my first experience with the process of editing, I confess having zero prior knowledge of the process. Whoa—what an experience! I acknowledge Donna Mazzitelli's insight and advice to make this effort increasingly better.

ABOUT THE AUTHOR

CAROL SCHAUER lives and works in Colorado, where she shares her home with her pooch. She enjoys being a homebody, endlessly DIY-ing, and also spending time with friends and family when opportunity strikes.